TAKE OFF YOUR SHOES

A Guide To The Nature of Reality

Stefan C. Nadzo

EDEN'S WORK
Publisher

Also By Stefan C. Nadzo

There Is A Way

For information contact:

Coleman Graphics, 99 Milbar Boulevard, Farmingdale, N.Y. 11735

Manufactured in the United States of America

Library of Congress Catalog Card Number 81-66185

ISBN: 0-937226-01-7

Cover design: *Centering,* an original oil painting by Nancy Russell Nadzo

EDEN'S WORK

*Happy is he who discovers Wisdom
        and who reaches Understanding,
For he finds Life.*

Proverbs

TAKE OFF YOUR SHOES

TABLE OF CONTENTS

AUTHOR'S NOTE

For those who like to plan ahead before setting out on an enterprise of any kind, who enjoy having an itinerary prepared by a travel agent prior to embarking on a journey from home, let us take a few moments to establish some ground rules for the discussion in these pages, to define some terms, and generally to share a sense of each other. We need not go into too much detail but just enough to provide an overview of more or less where we are headed and how we expect to get there. Those who are not procedurally minded and who prefer to take an uncharted course may want to choose to skip this foreword altogether and jump ahead into the text itself.

First, we should make it quite clear that this is a discussion. We are going to be asking ourselves about the nature of the universe and of our reality, seeking to understand something about who and what we are, and this is an area in which there really are no experts. If we do not understand the answers ourselves, and we can do that only by reaching them ourselves, they are not truly answers at all. So each of us has an equal stake in this effort, and our contribution to it must reflect that. Certainly, the focus of activity in any book seems to be on the writer while the reader simply absorbs, nodding in agreement or mumbling in disgust. But that is nowhere near a satisfactory description of what we are undertaking, and if that is all that occurs, then we both lose. While it might seem that I am in a controlling position, able to determine what goes into this inquiry and the direction it will take, that is no more than an appearance. Indeed, as I develop and pursue the thoughts and ideas included here, there will be many others which come to my mind but which will be excluded from the text for lack of space or time, or because I cannot find a way to put them into words. But nonetheless will I ruminate upon them as we go along, and I urge you to do the same with such points or concepts as may surface in your mind from time to time. When a thought arises which is not touched upon in the discussion, lay down the book, and follow its development in your own mind. Some in the sciences as well as other fields tell us today that our thoughts exist forever, and that there are ways we can retrieve or play back our own and those of others. If this is true, then possibly your tangential wanderings during this reading will intersect mine, to the eventual benefit of us both. In any case, I consider this effort a discussion, a mutual undertaking, not a lecture, and I hope that you will do so as well.

Secondly, I would emphasize that this is not intended to be a dispassionate inquiry. Our interest is not academic but intensely personal. We have joined forces here, in effect, to find out if there is more to our lives than just meeting the mortgage payments, and there is nothing sterile about that concern. If our discussion does not somehow change the image we see in the mirror, give to it more meaning and purpose, then we have gone nowhere. The underlying subject matter of this book is fraught with emotion, and we would probably not be together today had it not already brought us to tears more than once. We are here precisely because we have, each in his own way, come to realize that the question of our true nature is an important one, something we need to understand, and is, or at least may be, susceptible to our own efforts at answering it. And our emotions will be present -- anxiety, even anger, and hopefully some relief. That's all okay and to be expected. But the key is to express the emotions as they surface, and then to inquire of ourselves why a particular step found sensitive toes, and finally to move onward. In a discussion of this kind, there is no place for stone - walling, repression of feelings, or refusal to participate. By its nature, it will be personal; by ours, it can be productive.

Also, in an inquiry in which we are all at once experts and novices, there are bound to be some internal contradictions and inconsistencies. To the extent possible, of course, we will stay on one track and follow it, but inevitably some of what may be said at one point will seem (even be) inconsistent with what comes forth at another. That is in the nature of a discussion, and this is a discussion of the nature of reality seen as I see it now and put into those terms and constructions which seem now best to express that view. I reserve the right to change my mind, and you should do the same. We are seeking truth, and while the path from here to there is a straight one, we have done and will continue to do a lot of stumbling and wandering about in the traversing of it.

As to our itinerary, we will be looking in the first chapters at the way in which we seem to see and to react to our lives and at how that affects or determines our understanding of reality. We will focus briefly on the so - called scientific method for the development of knowledge in which many of us have been tutored, and we will try to determine the extent to which that is a useful process for this inquiry and whether or not we need feel bound by it. From our conclusions on these and related questions we will seek to establish a workable and practical understanding of the nature of reality. From that point, we will in succeeding chapters attempt to integrate our findings with the lessons of the New Testament. The teachings of Jesus of Nazareth are an inheritance shared by us all, especially in the West, but they are one with which many of us have serious difficulties of various kinds. Together, we will try to iron out some of those problem areas. By the time we are done here, we will I hope have opened up for each of us a whole new way of looking at ourselves and at the world around us such that we will quite literally be different persons as we close the book from those we were at its start. This is, to be sure, a tall order, but it is one which we can meet, if both of us genuinely wish it.

Now, let's look at some of the terms and constructions likely to arise and try to come to a more or less acceptable understanding of what we will mean by them. We have already mentioned "universe" and "reality", and no two may be so difficult and mercurial as these. Generally speaking, I will use the former to mean Creation; that is, the universe is Creation as seen by the Creator and therefore may (probably does) include elements or aspects of which we are totally unaware. The universe then is what is created. Reality, on the other hand, we might take to mean the universe as we see it: that which we perceive within us and outside us, including the act of perception itself. From the Creator's point of view, the universe and reality may be, likely are, one and the same, but from ours there might be a difference. Perhaps we can put it this way:

reality represents to us what we can, or think we can, grasp of the universe; it is our definition or description of the universe. In this way, our conception of the nature of reality may change as we change, but the universe remains constant. Unfortunately, we will almost certainly use the terms interchangeably now and again, especially in those areas where we are not aware of the difference between them -- that is, in those areas where our reality seems to us to be the universe as the Creator sees it. So long as we are aware of the risk, it should pose no real danger; but we must both remain alert to it.

Also, we are going to us the word "see" (in its various forms, including the idea of vision) in a way that is intended to go beyond the function of the physical eyes. We do that often in ordinary speech (as in, I see what you mean) but here we will be intending something beyond even that. The kind of vision and seeing we will be referring to is the process by which knowledge or understanding is reached without any apparent rational explanation. Some may prefer to call this intuitive knowledge as distinct from acquired knowledge. The important point is that it seems just to happen to us, as when an idea leaps to our awareness out of nowhere and prompts us to exclaim "Eureka!". We cannot explain the process by which it came to us, neither can we often describe exactly what it is we see. This kind of knowledge is non-transferable, transcending as it does the senses and the mechanics which process them. Many, if not all, religious and philosophical disciplines talk of this phenomenon. If you have experienced it, it is a part of your reality and you recognize its essential nature. If you have not experienced it, it will seem a meaningless idea; but it will, nonetheless, happen to you sooner or later, if you are prepared to let it happen.

"Truth" (with an upper case t) and "God" are terms which should be self-explanatory even though none of us knows exactly what either means. In this discussion, I will generally use the word God when I mean the Creator in His role as that (intending thereby neither to affirm nor deny that He may have other roles); those who prefer to use labels such as "the creative force" or "infinite intelligence", or some other are, of course, free to do so, and I urge you to read those where you see the word God. As to Truth -- it is that which we seek and which, from time to time, we *see*. The way we describe what we see will vary with each of us, depending upon our background, education, and perspective, and, to the extent that we are honest, we will then be imparting truth (in the lower case). Thus, truth can be different for each of us, but Truth (that which we have seen) is the same for all. It is, then, the descriptions which vary; there are many truths, one Truth. Also, we can say about Truth that once seen, it is easily and quickly recognized. While another's true explanation or description of it may seen laborious, complicated, and hard to grasp, the Truth itself is none of that. And in the sense that God as the Creator is too the Truth of Creation, we may use this term to mean that aspect of Him.

About the use of these and other words, it is important that, as in any communication between persons, we try to be as consistent and clear about their meaning as possible. On the other hand, much forward movement can be lost if we allow ourselves to get hung up over the selection of a particular word in preference to another in making a point. Clearly, we do not want to be sloppy, and we must make every effort to avoid that. But it is equally true that what we are dealing with here are ideas, ideas which some of us may never have really wrestled with before, and if we are to succeed at all we must feel free to let ourselves formulate them in any way we can. Once again, this is a discussion and is not intended to be a final product but rather a starting off point for continued searching, a catalyst to generate more questions suggesting alternative answers prompting additional questions.

Finally, in these times it is relevant to explain that the use of the masculine gender generally, in pronouns for the proper name God, and in terms like man in the sense of mankind, is a grammatical option imposed by the nature and limitations of the English language; the alternative construction he/she and its like seems unnecessarily complicated, and so I have chosen not to use it. None of us would be on this search for Truth, and certainly we would not be comfortable in it, if we carried with us as accompanying baggage the kind of prejudices and misconceptions which chauvinism of any variety generates. Jealous, belligerent, and blind attachment or devotion to any idea, concept, or circumstance clearly has no place in an inquiry of this kind, and to the extent that I know myself I bring none of it here.

A FEW FIRST WORDS

If we were told we could ask one question of God and be assured of a full and complete answer, I suspect that while each of us might word it differently, the question posed would be about the nature of our lives or of the universe. Who or what am I? Why or what am I? Who or What are You? Or, put somewhat more loosely, just exactly what is going on around here? And God would likely not be surprised at our choice of question because it is the very one which prompts us to set out on the quest for self-knowledge or spiritual awareness, to write or pick up a book like this one, and He has heard it, or will hear it, from all of us. If He were to show any surprise it might be because He has already provided us with the answer to this question over and over again in a variety of ways, through numerous mouths and by assorted pens. But it is the nature of the question that each has to find an answer for himself, and with luck we may be able to do some of that here, in these pages.

Early in the Old Testament of the Bible, a text used in its various forms by those of many traditions, cultures, and disciplines, we are told that among God's first words to Moses was the command that he remove his shoes, for he was, God said, standing on holy ground. Now, this event is reported to us as having occurred on the slopes of a mountain while Moses was alone tending a flock of sheep. We can assume that this was scruffy, rock-strewn terrain, not much good for anything but sheep (otherwise they would probably not have been allowed to graze on it), and upon hearing God's words, Moses, once he had regained his composure, may have very well looked about him at the weeds and droppings and murmured in disbelief, "Holy ground? This?" Remember too that in Moses' time, the appellation holy ground was likely reserved by the priests for sanctuaries, temples, and shrines, sites dutifully set apart, and this forsaken hillside was none of that. "Holy ground? You must be joking!"

We cannot know, of course, what exactly was God's point, but we can be certain, I think, that He was not joking. Also, it is likely, since the incident appears so early in the text, that God was speaking to Moses of first principles. That is, His message was intended to tell Moses, and the rest of us who would read of it later, something about the nature of the universe. And it could not have been an accident that God chose as the location for this particular lesson so unlikely a site as a mountain slope in the wilderness, the very kind of place to which the label holy ground would seem least appropriate. Perhaps what God wanted to put across was precisely the idea that wherever we are, at any time regardless of the surroundings or circumstances, we are standing on holy ground, or conversely, there is no ground on which we stand that is not holy.

Science seems today to be telling us that the universe is composed not, as we once thought, of many different substances in various categories of assorted kinds, but of one single element, or thing, or stuff, which simply seems to take different shapes and behave in different ways depending upon the conditions of the moment. Science calls this stuff energy. I may not have expressed this idea just as a scientist would, but it is more or less as I stated it, and the point is that everything, everywhere, is at base the same. Our universe is composed of one thing, energy, which manifests or expresses itself in different ways, but which is always the one thing it is. I submit that this concept is as much religious as it is scientific, and the greater the clarity with which we can bring ourselves to see the identity of these two too often conflicting approaches, the more evident will the truth of the hypothesis become for us, and the more applicable to our lives will we recognize God's first words to Moses. Because whether we say that everything is energy or everywhere is holy ground depends solely on our point of view; in either case we are saying something about the nature of the universe whose ramifications are awesome.

Now, most of us are inclined to leave these so-called esoteric and presumed highly intellectual concepts to the experts among us, be they priests, philosophers, or physicists. We assume that this is a subject too sacred, too deep, or too complicated for our understanding, and in any case not altogether relevant to our daily lives. Or, if we are not so easily cowed, and we acknowledge that it is too our business, we promise ourselves to focus on it at some point in the future when we are free of the responsibilities and duties of just plain living and have time to reflect on matters such as these. But the fact is, this *is* a matter of just plain living. If we are to be able to function coherently, effectively, and fruitfully in life, then clearly we need to know something about our nature and about the nature of the universe in which we seem to find ourselves. Nobody can find happiness in an environment he does not comprehend, whose nature and function he cannot relate to, or with. Surely the most miserable amongst us are those who understand least who they are; likewise, our least joyful moments are always those when we feel most foreign to our surroundings, physical, psychological, or spiritual.

Thus, God's first words to Moses can have an

application of momentous proportions to our lives whether we consider our orientation scientific or religious, and even in fact whether or not we seek to understand their meaning for us. Remember that the word holy comes from the same roots as the word whole, and in that sense we can understand God's message to mean that wherever we stand is all of creation, the whole universe. If we can understand that principle, we can understand our own nature and the nature of everything else. And of equal importance and significance is the complementary idea that *we* can reach that understanding. Standing on holy ground as we are wherever we are, we have only to look at ourselves and the soil beneath our feet (where we are at this moment), to understand all there is to know. We need not look to others for explanations, nor need we postpone our search. Our daily lives, for all their routine and mundane appearances, are manifestations or expressions of this first principle, and we can start looking for the answers to our questions about life just exactly where we are. Take off your shoes as a command from the Creator means that access to the truth of the universe is immediate. Im-mediate, that is, in its meaning that there need be no intervening medium or mediator, no agent or interval between us and the knowledge we seek about our lives.

The Nature of Things

What has brought us together in this book, I as writer and you as reader, is a shared and genuine interest in grasping something about what we are all about. Each one of us, of course, is driven by a particularly personal motive, perhaps a felt absence in our lives of meaning, happiness, direction, or satisfaction, and it is that which we hope to fill. But in the end, we all seek an answer to the same question, and that is, again, what's going on around here? Some may consider this a religious exercise, others prefer to label it scientific. My own bent, perhaps because of how I got to where I am right now, will seem more the former, but it really does not make much difference. We ought not to be interested in the religious explanation as such, nor in the scientific explanation, but in *the* explanation: the explanation that explains. Answers, not labels.

We are taught in mathematics that things equal to the same thing are equal to each other, and this rule applies to the search for the truth of things as well. Statements about the nature of things which are formed as earnestly and accurately as humanly possible are also equal to each other; they are identical statements, describing as they do the same thing, although they may seem different, even flawed, to those who arrived at the place by an alternate route. Thus, science's conclusion that everything is energy and religion's, as I have suggested it, that everywhere is holy ground are indeed the same observation said differently. It is the labels that confuse us, not the truth behind them, and we would do well to learn to see beyond labels in every aspect of our lives, but especially here. In commercial sales operations, the selection of a product's label is generally assigned to persons other than those who developed the product; and their choice of design will be predicated on market conditions and other factors which have little to do with the motives and purposes of the original inventor. But it is always the product which we use, not the label, and therefore it is at the product itself which we must look with scrutiny if we are to know the truth of it.

Early in my own search for the truth of things it became apparent, once I learned to see past the labels, that all the world's great teachings are the same. The perceived differences among religions and spiritual disciplines increasingly came to be recognized as just that, *perceived* differences, developed and perpetuated not by the teachers themselves but by those who followed. There is no convincing reason that I am aware of, for example, to believe that Jesus of Nazareth considered himself a Christian, or that Gautama Siddartha referred to himself as a Buddhist. These are labels that were assigned afterwards, and one wonders how the teachers would react to them; certainly, they have come, for many of us, to mean something very different from what the teachers taught. The lesson here is important if we are to understand for ourselves what our reality is all about. We have got to try to free ourselves of our attachment to and identification with labels, otherwise we will never recognize the product of our search, and the answer to our question, for what it is and what it is not.

Once again, the question each of us has asked is the same, and it is, I think, the same question asked by astronomy, biology, zoology, and theology: what is the nature of what I see, or, again, what's going on around here? If there is any difference whatsoever between the various -ologists and the rest of us, it is that their presence on this ground seems somehow more legitimate than our own, for they are the experts. But not any more. This is holy ground, and we are all barefoot here. Categorization of knowledge as scientific or religious surely has its place, and we are not quarreling with that practice; but for our purposes here it misses the point. We want to know what's going on, and we don't much care which drawer we find the answer in, so long as we find it for ourselves, and it answers.

Getting Underway

What we are undertaking here will not be easy. Identifying and understanding first principles never is, especially when we consider that in many ways we have strayed so far from this one. We are burdened by considerable confusion and even unhappiness in and about our lives, and all that will need to be sorted out. But having started, we have already taken the most difficult step, the first one, and while the rest will certainly not be all downhill, some degree of confidence in our eventual success is warranted. A little beyond the point in the Exodus story mentioned earlier Moses is told by God to free his people from slavery, and whether we choose to understand that literally or symbolically (that is, to free himself from the bondage of ignorance), and surely both interpretations are valid, we can take considerable encouragement from God's response to Moses' initial reluctance. Moses told God in effect that he felt inadequate to the task, and to this God replied that Moses need not fear for He would be with him. We should take that assurance to mean for us that as we pursue the same task, to free ourselves from our ignorance about our true nature, God is with us too. The forces of the universe are geared to facilitate our journey along this path; poised to spring into action. Not that we will succeed in a hurry, nor that it will take only one excursion, but we will prevail over whatever may seem to bind us. Despite the appearances, and they can be disquieting, the odds are heavily in our favor because what we seek is in the ground on which we stand and it is wherever we are; while we may have far to go, we have not far to look.

THE NATURE OF REALITY

We have suggested that perhaps the first question any of us asks on the search for the truth about Truth is, who or what am I? Or, what is the nature of the universe of which I seem to be a part? Or, again, as we put it a bit less formally, what's going on around here? Certainly, most religious scriptures begin with a discussion of this question, and science, which might be described as a religion of sorts, is prompted in the final analysis by a yearning for answers to this very inquiry. Indeed, it might be said that "who and what am I?" is the only question we ever ask, that every other question is simply this one said differently, and that if we ever develop an answer to this one we may never need to query anything again, for all else will be clear. And, conversely, we might be able to affirm that if we still harbor any unanswered questions about anything, we probably have not yet fully answered that first one, however confidently we may feel that we have done so. Presumably too it follows that there is only one correct answer to this basic question, but that there appear to be many because each of us, in our groping, voices his answer in words that reflect his point of view and state of development at the time of speaking, and in that respect we are all different. Thus, as we change our minds about which answer to this question makes sense to us, it is not the Truth about us that has changed but our perception and expression of it -- or, the place from which we view it. It is not inaccurate for a bird to say of a tree that it is branches and for a worm that it is roots. That is simply all that either sees of the tree, and both are correct for themselves even though neither can see the tree as the other does, nor would either one of them, so long as he looked from where he lives, understand the other's description of the thing.

So, in some ways at least, the answer to "who or what am I?" depends upon who and where I think I am at the moment of asking. And, by the act of asking the question, I change myself from a being who does not wonder about his nature to one who does, and in that change is already found part of the answer: I am a being who wonders about its nature. And, irresistibly, the more we wonder, the more we change. At first glance, this seems a circular process: the more I think about myself the more I think about myself. But actually it is less a circle than a spiral. The more we think about ourselves, the more our thinking changes and our perspective or field of vision broadens; and each time we look back at the subject of our inquiry, ourselves, we see it differently because it has changed into a being which has had new, additional, and different thoughts about itself. Let's go back to our worm for a moment -- as long as his curiousity about the nature of his universe remains unaroused, his sense of a tree will continue to be just roots; but the instant he wonders whether or not there might be more to a tree than that, he will change his perception of the thing and therefore its nature for him (from just roots to something which might possibly include more than roots). And the next time, after a rain, that he comes to the surface for air with this question about trees in his head, we might observe that the trunk towering above him is attached to or a part of the familiar roots below. He had, of course, seen the trunk before on previous rainy days, but now, prompted by his awakened curiosity about the nature of trees and roots, he has seen it differently. His question has prompted him to wonder, and his wondering has brought him to see the connection between the trunk above and the roots below, a connection that was always there but which he had never before observed because he had never thought about it. Now, having acknowledged that his customary understanding of roots and trunks was, if not wrong, at least incomplete or limited, he might find himself looking at everything differently, wondering if perhaps other apparently separate or isolated aspects of his world are not also connected to each other, just as he found roots and trunks to be. And, as he discovers more connections of these kinds, might he not perhaps one day wonder whether or not he could apply this new, expanded perception to himself? If roots and trunks are actually two aspects of one whole, as he has seen them to be, might that suggest to him something about his own nature -- is he connected to or a part of something else too?

So, from his initial, apparently innocent question about the nature of trees, our underground friend has started himself out on a quest for knowledge which will lead him to seek out an understanding of the whole universe itself. And his eventual, final answer may be no different from his first; that is, as roots and trunks are connected, so is everything else, and thus in his new knowledge of trees resides all he will ever learn, although of course he will not recognize that until he has gone the full route.

In The Image of God

Almost every, perhaps even every, religious scripture tells us in effect that we have been created in the image of God, that our True nature is God - like; surely there is more in that coincidence than just accident. Perhaps if we look at this idea from a somewhat unorthodox angle it will help to shed some light on it. There is, as our worm's experience should suggest, often considerable and sometimes unexpected benefit gained from looking at a thing in a way entirely different than is customary. Not only may we thereby see in the thing aspects previously hidden from our view but also, and perhaps more importantly, we acquire a new appreciation of the process of observation itself.

What we believe about the nature of reality (what we think to be real) depends very largely on the image we have about the existence and nature of a Creator. Even the apparent absence of such an image is reflected in our outlook on the world around us. We cannot separate our impressions of Creation from those we have of its Creator; indeed, if they are not the same thing, certainly they are two sides of the same thought. In a very real sense, we can say that our reality, or our sense of it, stems from or is directly related to the image we have of God. And as our view of ourselves changes (through the process of inner seaching and discovery) so will our understanding of God; we cannot alter our view of any creation, be it ourselves, the world, or a ceramic pot, without altering our understanding of its creator, and vice versa. In this sense, can we not then say that we are created (exist at least in our own minds) in the image -- that we have -- of God?

Does that admitted word-game contradict the

teaching that we are created in the image of God? Indeed not, for He could have created us as He saw Himself (Perfect, Loving, and Whole) and still left us free to see ourselves differently (confused, cantankerous, and separate), and free to see Him as like us (vengeful, jealous, and playing favorites). To be sure, our view of Him cannot change the way He sees Himself, nor can our view of ourselves change the way He sees us. But if the way He sees Himself determines the way He sees us (as in His image) then what is true for Him must be true for us as well. Therefore, if we wish to see ourselves more as we likely are (as we were created rather than as we now seem or think ourselves to be) then perhaps it follows that one way to do that is to try to see our Creator as He sees Himself by seeking to see ourselves as He sees us. This too may seem a circular exercise, but as a tool for self-discovery its thrust is definitely upward; and the centrality of its application to our discussion will become increasingly apparent as we go along. At this point though it is enough to recognize that we cannot wonder about the nature of the universe, as we are doing, without wondering too about its Creator, for our thoughts about either one will reflect and be reflected in our thoughts about the other.

Asking the Question, Why?

Telos is a Greek word, and its meaning has something to do with seeking to understand the why of things. So that, for example, if we ask why birds sing, the telic response is that they do so to attract a mate or to establish their territory or whatever. And most of us spend much of our lives in a fruitless search for the telic answer to everything. Each of us can, I expect, identify with the tired parent who eventually responds to a child's incessant "Why?" with a frustrated, final "Just because". We can identify with it because we have been there, but still we sense that it is an unfair and incomplete answer. Or is it?

Consider the common squirrel for a moment. We have all been taught that a squirrel works the summer and fall collecting nuts and other good things, storing them in a secret place for the long, cold winter ahead. Indeed, this activity of that furry little rodent is frequently held up to us as an example we too should follow: plan now for the rainy day to come, let today's effort be for tomorrow's harvest.

But is the coming winter really the reason that the squirrel so feverishly builds his cache? Or is it just possible that the squirrel collects and stores nuts in the summer and fall precisely, and only, because that is what a squirrel is: an animal that collects and stores nuts in the summer and fall? Perhaps winter is the farthest thing from his mind as he scurries up a tree to deposit yet another mouthfull of acorns in a branch cavity. Perhaps he never even thinks about winter at all; but when winter does come, we can amend our definition to include: a squirrel is an animal that eats nuts and acorns stored in a secret place. So, a squirrel does what he does because it is his nature to do it, not for any telic reason we might develop about him. After all, surely we cannot suggest that winter comes because a squirrel stores nuts!

What this possible nonsense about squirrels and nuts has to do with this discussion is that early on we might do well to agree not to ask ourselves the why of creation, trying to square its apparent inconsistencies with our inevitably inadequate answers, and acknowledge instead, at least for now, that what is is because that is the nature of things. Let us direct our attention, then, not at why the universe was created (not try to psychoanalyse God, as it were) and instead concentrate our efforts on seeking to understand how our reality is formed (that is, the process by which we come to think of ourselves as we do). Certainly, the why of it will always be in our minds for it seems to be in our nature to wonder about that, but shifting our focus from there to the how can simplify our task, at least at this stage. Simply stated, we cannot understand the why of a thing until we understand what it is!

The Laws of Nature and Science

Words can be heavy things, and the word law is one of the heavier among them. After all, a law is something none of us wants to be in violation of, and if there is any danger that this discussion may be leading us in that direction, we want to be aware of that now.

In this search to fathom the nature of reality we rightly expect, I think, to discover laws which are, among other possible characteristics, immutable, constant, clear, and possibly even simple (in the sense of uncomplicated or fully distilled). Too, we can assume that these laws will be true and effective wherever, whenever, and by whomever applied. Indeed, we may even say of them that they must be fully in force whether or not any of us is aware of their existence. That is, they can be presumed to govern reality regardless of what we think of them or whether or not we think of them. Remember, we are talking about basics here: the answer to my question, who or what am I?, if it is the true answer, must be true also about you and about everyone and everything else, with no qualifiers. Otherwise, it is not a law about the nature of the universe but a qualified observation -- an observation about me, for example, which depends on others meeting all the subjective conditions of me at the time of observation in order to be applicable to them as well.

A law, then, is objective, free of conditions, qualifiers, and exceptions.

What can we say in this connection about the laws of science, and to what extent must we feel bound by them in our search? If we apply the standards just suggested, it seems evident that they are not laws at all, but observations. To be sure, it is okay for men of science to use the word law to describe their conclusions, just so that we know what is meant by that use. In effect, what a particular scientist does, for example a student of homo sapiens, is to look in a mirror -- albeit augmenting his field of vision with various sophisticated devices and techniques -- and describe what he sees. Or, if his expertise is in another field, he moves from a mirror to a window, but still he describes what he sees "out there".

We are all familiar with the numerous historical instances in which this morning's laws of nature as expounded by science are erased and replaced by new knowledge gathered this afternoon; and the additional information which rendered erroneous and obsolete the old law generally speaking, if not always, springs from a change in perspective represented by the development of a more powerful instrument, for example, or the relaxation of some institutional taboo. Thus we can say that while the earth may never have been the center of the solar system despite the law which once so dictated, from man's point of view at the time, that is the way things *seemed* to be and therefore, for all he knew then, were. The observation, as an observation, was fully valid when and under the conditions in which it was reached, just as the current, revised observation about the solar system is equally valid for its time. An observation then is a description, and is entirely dependent upon who is seeing, when, and with what.

What this means for us is simply that we need not feel discomfited, or allow ourselves to be threatened **by** the discomfiture of others, if in our search we gather impressions or develop conclusions which seem to violate what we understand to be the current set of scientific laws. From the point of view of a practising medical doctor, if one pierces his skin with a nail, bleeding will result; from the point of view of an accomplished fakir, that will not be the case. Both men are correct from their point of view. At this moment, we need feel bound by neither.

A Child's Dragons

Consider a child put to bed and left for the night in a darkened room: unable to sleep, he looks about him, and suddenly out of the closet he sees a fire-breathing dragon, in a corner a rampant bear, against a wall a hangman's noose, and crawling out from under the bed vicious serpents. Quite naturally, and surely this or its like has happened to each of us, he is frightened and lets out a frantic call for his mother who leaves her dinner guests and, upon entering the boy's room to see what is amiss, turns on the light. In an instant, the menacing beasts are seen by the child not to be dangerous at all, and more, they are seen not to have even been beasts, but instead an empty coat-hanger left on the closet doorknob, a sweater thrown carelessly over the back of a chair, the shadow of a tree against a wall, and, as for the vicious reptiles, well, he sees there is nothing there at all. But at the time they certainly seemed to be there, every bit as real and frightening as the cry for help suggested.

Perhaps the world we live in is something like the child's darkened room. Our abiding sense of insecurity and anxiety about poverty, loneliness, the impermanence and unpredictability of life, all these and more, may be born of a variety of fear inducing and sustaining "things" -- ideas, thoughts, impressions, conclusions, doctrines -- which, when the light of knowledge is turned on, may be seen not only not to have been fearful but even not to have been real, at least not as they appeared to us in the dark. All of our current understanding of the world, then, might be suspect, and should be acknowledged as subject to revision and possibly relinquishment. This admission does not demand that we start out by flailing ourselves with guilt about being misguided or wrong, but it does require that we be open and receptive to the prospect of having been misguided and wrong. The child is not punished for having seen dragons but merely, gently with love, corrected.

At the risk of treading on thin ice (and much of the time here we will be doing just that), we might develop the darkened room analogy further to wonder if, even as he is overwhelmed by the apparent reality of the beasts all about him, the child -- in his "heart" -- knows that the dragon is only a coat-hanger, the bear a misplaced sweater, knows that what he had allowed himself to become convinced of is not really true. And if that can be said of the child, can it be said of us? Do we already have the knowledge we are seeking, and are we not perhaps engaged less in an effort of learning than of unlearning? After all, the child's light was on when he first went to bed. Was ours too?

A Brief Look at Miracles

A moment ago we mentioned the fakir who can pierce his skin with a nail without blood loss, and I am sure that each of us has seen on television or read of similar cases in which the apparently impossible has been performed. If these kinds of events seem religious in nature, the world labels them miracles, and if not, then aberrations. As we have agreed that the choice of labels is simply a reflection of one's point of view, we need not concern ourselves with which is the more appropriate; either way we are acknowledging the possibility of exceptions to the rule, and the implications of that are obvious. However, these kinds of events themselves should be of interest to us because they may tell us something about the nature of reality, which is our focus.

Is it not possible that what is at work in the performance of these phenomena is the application of entirely different sets of standards about the universe? Certainly, it is evident that we label an event such as the one described "miraculous" or whatever precisely because it contradicts our present understanding of the universe. Remember our earlier discussion of telic reasoning, and our decision no longer to ask the why of things. Thus, from our non-telic point of view, we can say that blood flows not because skin is pierced, but rather that it is in the nature of the universe as we currently understand it that blood flows from skin pierced by a nail. If blood flow does not materialize under those conditions, we then say that our understanding of the universe has been superseded or negated, and we call the event miraculous. But is it seen as miraculous by the one performing the event? Or is it possible that he simply has a different understanding of the nature of the universe to which the absence of blood flow under those conditions conforms absolutely, and therefore what is cause for awe or alarm to us is to him merely the manifestation of the ordinary? And if, to continue with this example, the fakir could somehow teach us to understand, adopt, and practice the perspective he employs in his life, could we too then pierce our skin with a nail without consequent blood loss, and not see the event as miraculous? Indeed, if that were the case, it might then be exceptional if blood did flow!

If this brief discussion of the nature of miracles is anywhere near the mark, what can we learn from it? Perhaps we should recognize in the performance of miracles by others among us evidence confirming what we have already begun to suspect: that the nature of reality and of the universe itself depends, in an as yet unclear way, on our individual point of view or understanding of it. What we expect to happen under any given set of circumstances will happen precisely because we expect it; and conversely, what we absolutely do not allow as possible will not happen. This may explain why some experience miracles in their lives and others never do. In any case, perhaps one of the purposes of miracles is simply to flag to our attention the limits of our current understanding of the universe. Miracles may not be so much extraordinary events as they are suggestions to us of what, from a changed point of view, the nature of reality might be -- and of how we can or should (not in a moral, but a practical, lesson-learned sense) see the world.

How does this conclusion square with most religious teachings that miracles are instances of intervention in our lives by God directly or through his emissaries? Possibly very nicely, if we recall our earlier suggestion that God sees us as like Himself (again, created in His image); His performance of miracles among us then might simply be His way of alerting us to how we might see the universe (as He does) if we would only choose to do so. Remember too that we said that He permits us the freedom to see ourselves and our world as we like, and, presumably, to accept the consequences of that choice.

The Nature of Things

We seem to be coming to an inescapable conclusion that reality has no characteristics or aspects which are true for all people under all conditions. The nature of things seems to depend in some definite if undefined way on what we think about them, how we view them, and where we are standing at the moment of observation. The world seems, or is, flat until we look at it differently, and then it seems, or is, round. We have all read of medical experiences in which patients who expect their condition to worsen and who lose their will to live fare less well from a healing point of view than those who have a more positive outlook. Again, expectations seem to govern reality. The more we search for constancy, immutability, and predictability, the more, it seems, we come up with just the opposite. If one man's extraordinary and impossible are indeed just another's routine and likely, then where are we left in our quest for permanent, clear, and simple rules about the nature of reality? Having discarded all the so-called laws as no more than personal or institutional points of view valid only for those who adopt them, and only for so long as they do, are we then left standing at the edge of the universe holding an empty bag? If so, then the prospect is so unsatisfying (not to mention terrifying) that we were probably better off with the bagful we had, inadequate as its contents may have been. But if the only way we can discover predictability in the universe is by accepting the standards and observations of others, and remain always willing to change our minds as they change theirs, then the nature of reality becomes nothing more than another manifestation -- the ultimate manifestation, perhaps -- of the jungle principle that might makes right. Whoever is the loudest, strongest, and most convincing among us is permitted to determine, even dictate, for the rest how the universe will be understood. Unless, in the very impermanence and relativity that we seem to have uncovered, there lie constancy and predictability.

The Creator made the universe and saw that it was good, we are told. To be sure, we cannot know exactly what was meant by His use of the word good, but perhaps we can assume that He intended more than that word has come commonly to suggest -- more than tasty, sensually satisfying, fun, or amusing. Indeed, I expect -- and here again I am stepping onto thin ice -- we can conclude that good in the Genesis sense includes some of the characteristics we hoped to find in our search for universal laws: constancy, predictability, and consistency -- that is, following a pattern or plan. If we are right, or even partly right, in this interpretation of God's use of the word, and if we can assume, as we must, that He could not have been mistaken, then we can say, as it seems that He did, that the nature of things is good, or, put somewhat differently, that it is in the nature of things to be good, or, again, that it is in the nature of things that good occurs. That is, the nature of the universe (the occurrence of events and the performance and characteristics of things) is good: constant, predictable, and consistent. I recognize that we seemed, only a moment ago, to have concluded just the opposite, but stay with me another thought or so anyway to see if this apparent contradiction will iron itself out.

Let us go back just a bit and recall that God created us in His image, in the nature of Him, and therefore what He saw as good (consistent and predictable), so can we; and if we do not do so, as so far we seem not to have done, perhaps it is because we are looking at the thing, the universe, wrongly, or at least differently from the way He looks at it. He was satisfied with His Creation, He saw that it was good, presumably because He saw that things were where, and functioning as, He intended. Let us now discover if we can see them that way too.

Perhaps the key lies in the idea that God saw that things function as they were intended to function. Quite simply, we have seen that the universe seems to conform to our beliefs about it -- our flesh spills blood from a nail puncture because we expect it to do so, a fakir's doesn't because he doesn't. Perhaps that is exactly the way God created the thing. Perhaps He created the universe in just such a way that it would conform to our beliefs about it! It conformed to His beliefs about it we are told (He saw that it was good), and we are further told that He created us like Him, in His image, so possibly it follows that the universe must, by its nature, conform to our beliefs about it (again, as it did to

29

His, Whom, we are like). If you can see the sense in this, which you will if you open your mind to it, then it will become apparent that our beliefs and expectations are absolutely crucial, and that for an understanding of reality we must look inward, at ourselves, not outward, at things.

It is in the nature of things that good occurs. What that statement could mean for us is that whatever occurs does so because we want or expect it to happen. Not because we make it happen (in a cause-effect sense) but because that particular occurrence, whatever it might be, is an aspect of or conforms to the universe as we believe it to be, for the universe is created, or programmed, to conform to our beliefs about it. So, if for example we look about us and see misery, illness, famine, and strife, perhaps they exist as they do, not because they are the inescapable lot of man, but because we believe in a universe in which misery, illness, famine, and strife are the inescapable lot of man. And the way to rid ourselves of those discomforts is not to build more hospitals, grow more corn, or enlist more policemen, not to seek to effect change outwardly, but to alter our beliefs about the universe, to change inwardly.

We may be living, then, in a universe in which our every wish, our every belief about it, is fulfilled. Again, not as a result of our having wished it, but by virtue of the fact that we wish it; the wish for something presupposes its existence and may even be its existence. But who, we might object, wishes for misery or illness? And the answer, of course, is that we all do; by *believing* in a universe of which misery and illness are a part, we are granted such a universe. (Although they may not be synonymous, substituting the word wish for believe may help you get a handle on this idea.) Seek and you shall find, we have been taught; if that is true about anything, it must be true about everything: whatever you seek, you will find. And, conversely, whatever you find, you can be sure you were seeking, whether or not you realized you were. That may very well be the nature of the universe God created and gave to us. The importance of realizing what it is we are seeking, of knowing ourselves, becomes of paramount significance. How many of the world's teachers have been trying to tell us that -- know thyself -- over the centuries!

The Universe as Plutonic

To understand the nature of reality, we must understand ourselves, because our reality is ourselves made manifest. The individual, personal responsibility of that assertion is awesome, but it does meet the standards for a law which we set. It is constant, immutable, and simple. And it works, always, everywhere, and by whomever applied.

In geology, the term plutonic means something like: the shape or characteristics of a formation are dependent upon, are a direct reflection of, the activity of molten rock beneath the surface; shifts or changes on the outside are caused by or result from shifts or changes on the inside. (And here the idea is what I am after, so I ask the forebearance of any geologists among us.) The one and the other are inexorably linked; indeed, they are the same event. And so it is with the universe. What God is determines what He can create and what He sees. And what is true of God is true of us too, for we are created like Him. Therefore, as we think we are, so is our reality (what we think the universe to be). The inner and the outer are one and the same, plutonic. What we are, we see. As we are inwardly, so our world is. Now, take a look about you: what you see is what you are. The universe is keyed to its creator; our reality is keyed to us. That is the nature of things. So, we must not look to others to effect changes in a world we dislike because it is we who must change first, from within. What we see outside will follow suit. This idea may not come easily to you, but wrestle with it anyway for it can explain everything. We will be working with it together a lot more in the pages ahead, and it will become clearer as we go along.

We live in a plutonic universe. A universe created by God which reflects what we think about ourselves; and as we have seen, that is reflected by, may even be the same thing as, what we think of Him. So, again as we said earlier, if we wish to see the universe as He sees it, if we wish our reality to be the same as His, we must strive to see ourselves (to recognize that we are) as He sees us and to see Him as He sees Himself. Let us on earth see as it is seen in Heaven -- Perfect, Whole, and Loving. So He is; so are we, for we were created like Him, if we would but see ourselves that way. The promise is His; the responsibility and the challenge to fulfill it are ours.

The Prism Effect

We must seek to see God as He sees Himself and ourselves as He sees us, as in His image, if we are to see ourselves as we are. And yet, so long as we consider Him a being, or Being, *separate* from us, a some-thing to be seen, an object for an observer to observe, we doom ourselves to failure. For the point may well be that it is the very idea of separation, with which we identify so dearly, that is itself the obstacle to our seeing correctly. So long as we insist on looking at Him as if from afar, a stance which has unfortunately come to seem less a choice than a fact of life, we remain blind to His true nature, and thus to our own. In a universe in which there is only one substance, be it energy or being-ness or Life, any hypothesis which suggests or depends upon separativeness misses the mark completely and leads its adherents ever further from the truth.

But if the universe does indeed consist of only one essence or stuff, how can it have happened that we, as creatures of that unitary creation, could be so confused about its nature? How is it possible in an ordered and perfect, that is, error-free, universe, as it is described by both science and religion, that any aspect of it, in this case us, could see it erroneously? How can we be wrong about a creation which is by definition right, a creation of which we are an aspect? How, finally, can a thing see itself as it is not? Maybe this dilemma is what The Fall is all about.

Part of the difficulty with the traditional concept of The Fall may be that it has become for us much more, and much less, than its original, intended message. It has become so heavily laden with ponderous moral implications that all we can derive from it is an overriding and blinding sense of guilt. Rather than learn from it, we seek instead to be punished for it, or, at least, to assume that we ought to be. Seeing the Creator as we see ourselves, we assume that He is disappointed and angry at our having "fallen", and, wanting to please Him Whom we love (or fear), we hate ourselves for failing Him. None of that is going to assist us in understanding what is truly going on. But suppose the Biblical account of The Fall was intended not as an account of God's displeasure with His creation but rather as an explanation of how we came to see ourselves as we are not. Perhaps it is a lesson, not an accusation, and its purpose is to facilitate our growth, not to excuse our punishment. I would suggest that The Fall story may be, albeit among other things, another way of telling us that the universe is plutonic. Recall, after all, that in all versions of this incident it was Adam and Eve, or their other-culture counterparts, who *chose* to disobey, and were apparently free to do so. Had the Creator really intended to forbid the event, as in an irreversible and unappealable veto, certainly He was capable of arranging that. Indeed, what the story should convey to us is the advice so many of us have given our own children: please do as I say for, believe me, your father knows best. And, true to course, our children too go off willy - nilly, often to their later regret, but eventually to work it out with our freely offered loving help. Just as we are doing now, with His.

Adam and Eve knew their true nature when they chose to ignore it, but having known it, they likely remember being told not to forget it, just as the child in the darkened bedroom we spoke of probably knew all the while he was screaming for help that the beasts were not beasts and the room was really quite safe. Why he would choose to see beasts where there were none and drive himself up the wall with fear, we cannot know -- that may be part of the telic mire we have agreed to sidestep. But perhaps we can decipher *how* it might have happened, how one aspect of a unitary creation might have come to see itself and all the rest as not one, but many.

Consider the simple prism, an ordinary piece of multifaceted glass. As any schoolboy knows, if we hold a prism up to a source of white light and view the light through the glass, what was a single color will suddenly be seen quite differently: as a spectrum of separate, distinct colors. What was one (the single color white) now appears as many (purple, blue, green, yellow, orange, and red). Explaining this phenomenon in the classroom, we say that the prism has refracted or broken down the white light into its component parts. But, having said that, we must take care not to conclude that the parts exist independently of the whole; that is, the colors are not themselves separate, self-sustaining things which exist apart from the white light. They are not really parts at all; they are aspects of the whole and inseparable from it. The individual, *apparently* separate colors are just another way of seeing the one white light. Indeed, they are white light, seen differently. The spectrum purple-through-red is not a thing of itself but simply white viewed through a prism, and to demonstrate that point we have only to remove the prism and the "other" colors disappear. They never really could exist at all without the white light, and they certainly were not separate entities, although in the glass they seemed to be. Again, the apparent separate and distinct reality of the spectrum is created by the prism (one color seen as many). During our use of the prism, the white light is not itself actually changed, does not cease to exist as it was before or after our use of the prism, and in a very real sense, it is all that was ever really there.

Once again without seeking to understand why it might occur, suppose that one aspect of Creation were to hold up before its "eyes" a similar prism and then view itself and the rest through that piece of glass. Instantly, the One would be seen as many. The Whole, artificially broken down into its apparent component parts, would suddenly look to the viewer as separate, varied, and distinct elements. Where there had been just white, there would now seem to be purple, blue, green, yellow, orange, and red. The One would not have *become* many, but it would appear as many (just as white light does not become the spectrum, it is *seen* as a spectrum). And, continuing with this illustrative device, suppose our viewer forgot for a moment that he was looking through a prism (perhaps in his fascination with the colors); he might eventually forget the exercise altogether and come to believe that the colors are real in and of themselves, that they are all that there is, and that the image created by the prism is not just a refraction of something else but the universe itself. The universe would then be seen not as the single source light that it is, the one stuff which is creation, as in "Let there be light", but as the spectrum which it seems to be. What is one is now -- appears to be -- many, and as the prism itself is forgotten, so is the source and nature of the spectrum, and we come to accept as self-sufficiently real and complete what isn't either. (Those familiar with the chakra, or powerpoint, concept will recognize in the prism effect spectrum the colors corresponding to those points; there may be more to that similarity than coincidence.)

One immediately evident flaw in this illustration lies in the fact that it assumes a subject, the viewer, using some kind of instrument, a prism, to look at an object, everything else. The problem, of course, is that the viewer is himself part of what he is seeing in the prism; that is, we are seeing ourselves incorrectly as well as everything else. The subject-object relationship of a viewer looking through a prism at a light source is easy enough to imagine, but we cannot so easily paint a mental picture of a subject looking at itself in that way, a subject-subject relationship. The dualistic nature of our thought process which interprets everything separatively in subject-object terms precludes our grasping a subject-subject relationship, and may itself be a product of the prism effect. We think that way because the parameters we accept for our minds themselves grew out of our employment of the prism. As we see the universe, we see ourselves, and if we assume the one to be limited and separative, then so do we see the other. One equally flawed way to get around this flaw in the illustration might be to consider the glass not as being between the viewer and the viewed but as a prismatic mirror, whatever that may be. Then we might imagine the One, or an aspect of the One, looking in the glass and seeing itself in the refracted reflection as many.

In any case, with all its shortcomings, the prism effect construction does at least serve to suggest the nature of the problem before us. Virtually all the great spiritual or religious teachers, and others who might not include themselves in that category but who have nonetheless attempted to decipher life's mysteries, seem to arrive, if by various routes, to a common conclusion that somehow we are seeing the universe as it is not, that we are neither what nor where we think we are, and that from that first error of perception spring our difficulties, confusion, and discomfort. Clearly, if that is the case, all of our efforts to adapt to our perceived environment --

psychological, physical, and social -- are bound to fall short, generating ever-increasing frustration and renewed, equally doomed attempts to fit in. Having started off on the wrong foot and headed in the wrong direction, we simply cannot get into step or flow with the universe unless and until we start over. It is not, apparently, so much that we have not yet found our own drummer and that we are listening to the wrong one as it is that we do not hear the only one there is. Let them see who have eyes to see is a lesson found in practically every discipline, and since we all obviously have eyes, the reference surely is to a different kind of seeing, a different set of eyes, than we have come to rely upon. Perhaps the reference is to eyes that can see the prism for what it is, and beyond it, and surely the first step toward that accomplishment is to recognize that we may be victims and products of our own error, of the prism effect.

Or, said somewhat differently, in a plutonic universe in which we are promised to experience what we expect to experience, we have got to deal first with our expectations, and clearly they are directly a function of our beliefs about the nature of reality. We cannot expect what we cannot conceive of, and we can conceive of only what we believe to be possible or likely -- that is, as falling within the bounds or limits of reality as we believe it to be. To alter our reality, then, we have to alter our understanding of what is possible; we have to see the universe totally differently than we do now, otherwise everything that comes to us will simply be more of the same. As the saying goes, the more things change, the more they are the same; and this is true, will remain true, so long as changes are effected within the old framework. It is not our attitudes or actions that are the fault, although they are telling symptoms, but our point of departure. Again, we have got to start over, from the beginning, for it is at the beginning that there was light.

THERE WAS A MAN

Incredible as it may at first seem, there was a man who is a familiar figure to every reader of this book, whose life and thoughts have shaped the destinies of countless millions, around whom numerous world religious movements have been developed, *and* who saw and described the universe exactly as we have done, at least as I read him. To be sure, many might argue with this interpretation of the teachings, but the fact remains that a fresh, objective reading of the material about him leads one almost unavoidably to this somewhat shakening and highly exhilarating conclusion. Shakening because the man is, of course, Jesus of Nazareth, and however much adulthood may assume fearlessness, we all of us still live a bit in dread of the Sunday-school instructor's scowl and rod; and exhilarating because so much of what was forced down us as youths and often made no sense, and clearly was being ignored by so many around us, finally does make sense. The man to whom so many pay ready lip service and so few any genuine attention; whose story has certainly seemed at best a highly fictionalized or embellished legend and at worst sheer mythology; who as an individual appeared weak, unconvincing, unrealistic, and even ridiculous -- a way out for idealists and escapists, but hardly relevant to the rest of us achievers; this man about whom perhaps more has been said and less understood than any other, including it should be noted possibly even in this treatment, can emerge from the dust and cobwebs of our personal attics as nothing short of brilliant.

I said a new reading of the material about this man would bring one to this conclusion, and I urge upon every earnest seeker such an undertaking. For starters, I suggest an edition of the New Testament that is different from, and thus unencumbered by, our Sunday-school experience. There are, of course, many on the market today, and for this purpose the best may be the one we have heard least about. The point is to approach the story as if for the first time and as if we had never before heard anything about it or about the man. Consider it, in this instance, not as the unimpeachable utterings of divinely inspired instruments (all of which it may very well be), but as simply one seeker's guide to other seekers -- one man's view of the spiritual struggle and search passed on to those he knew were trailing along behind. Looked at from this point and in this way, the Gospel accounts are unsurpassed in relevance and merit, and the man's teachings can be seen to have been and to be almost unbelievably clear, concise, consistent, sensible, and simple. And right on the mark. Everything they never before seemed to be, and more.

What's In A Name

Many traditions teach that if we name a thing, we can come to know it, for a thing's name is its nature. But it is also true about names that once we have attached an understanding of a thing to the name we have given it we seem to experience considerable dfficulty if we ever need or wish to see the thing differently. And sometimes this resistance can become downright insurmountable, even crippling. A name is a thing's nature, or at least comes to be it, partly because we thoroughly associate the two with each other whether or not it makes good sense or logic to do so. A rose by another name *would* smell differently, because much of the sweetness and pleasure derived from the odor stems from our association with the word rose, and that has less to do with the plant itself than with our own backgrounds and personalities. Likewise, the pejorative labels we use for other nationalities and racial groups tell us much more about ourselves than about their targets, and to change our view of others we often must first change the labels we apply to them.

The name Jesus is just such a label. As a word it has become for many of us fraught with meaning and energy which far exceed its purpose or value as simply a way by which to identify this man from other men. Few of us can utter or read the word without invoking much more than just an image of a first century figure. This phenomenon can be employed to good advantage on our search for truth, but it can also act as a terrible hindrance to progress for those who, because of their formal religious upbringing or other associations with the word, can barely bring themselves to voice the name without discomfort or embarrassment. For this reason, I propose that we address the man in this inquiry not by his name but in his role as a seeker and a teacher. It is from that perspective that we want to draw from the New Testament at this time, and it follows that we should look at him in that way too. I hasten to note that we do not intend by this device to tamper with the nature of the man himself, but only to effect an emotional defusing for those for whom the name itself may be an obstacle to forward movement.

The Man And The Prism

As I suggested at the outset of this chapter, what may be the most remarkable product of a fresh reading of the New Testament is a conclusion that the man seems to have been saying about reality very nearly exactly what we here have said, if infinitely better than we. And what we are now going to try to do is translate some of his lessons into our language and, I suspect, be surprised at the fit. For this endeavor, we will look primarily to the first book of the New Testament, but other areas of the Bible are borrowed from too. And, of course, it must be reemphasized that we are here interested in the man as a seeker and a teacher, and it is primarily in those roles that we will be looking at him. Whatever else he may have been, our major focus will rest there. Additionally, we must remember too that if he saw the universe as I am suggesting he did (as we here have begun to do), then whenever he taught, his eye would have been on the Truth as it is, on the "other" side of the prism we spoke of, even though his audience saw him and themselves as very much on "this" side, as part of and a product of the refraction. That is, if we are at least conceptually correct in what we said about the prism effect, we must assume that this New Testament teacher saw it too, if in different terms, and he would have intended his words to reflect and express that vision. Thus, even though he appeared to his listeners and is presented to us by many Biblical writers as a separate, distinct individual just as we think of ourselves (and they thought of themselves), his point always would have been and certainly seems to have been that he was not what he seemed and that neither are we. The fact is that his lessons, if properly understood and followed, will improve our lot in this world (on this side of the prism), but it is quite clear that his aspirations for us went far beyond that accomplishment. Yes, he hoped to show us the way to better, more fulfilling lives, but beyond that he wanted us to see why and how his teachings about Truth could have that happy effect -- because it is in our seeing that the change must take place and will be evidenced. As the man himself said, he was in this world, that is, as we see it now, but not *of* it, and I believe he wanted us to see ourselves that way too. His lessons, then, were not so much a prescription as they were, and are, a statement about the nature of reality, a statement which could and will change our lives totally but only if we will seek to see it that way. Likewise, his assertion that the Creator and he are one was likely much more than the presentation of credentials that we generally interpret it to have been. Surely it was an expression of Truth that the apparent many (he as an individual, we as individuals, and every*thing* else) are one, that what lies beyond the apparency, beyond the prism, is all that there is. Not separate, not many, but One.

Finally in our preparation for a new look at this teacher's lessons, we would do well to acknowledge that it is clearly not the story of just one man. It is the story of every man. Just as many of the individual lessons themselves are presented to us in parable form, so can the full account of the man's life itself be seen as a parable for us. His birth, the events in his life, and his death, are as accurate a representation of what lies ahead for each of us on this search as they are simply a presentation of one man's experience along the universal way. And we detract nothing from the beauty and historicity of the story by looking at it too from his highly personalized perspective; indeed, it is clear from many of his words that the man himself intended and hoped that we would do just that. He was a man, but too, as he told us, he was the way, and we should not hesitate to see him and his story as that, for in doing so are we better enabled to understand where we are, where we have been, and to anticipate what lies ahead along our own passage of the way. He is at once a guide and a map, and we should use him as both.

Unless We Become Like Children

Not long after the Old Testament conversation referred to in the opening of this book, God is quoted as telling Moses that He will visit the iniquity of the fathers on their children and on their children's children. For many of us, this attitude has seemed untenable in a Creator said to love His creation, but if we reconsider it in the context of a universe that is plutonic, it comes out rather more comprehensible. You will remember that in the last chapter we concluded that our reality is determined or shaped by the way we choose to see it, and that a change in the latter is reflected in the former. Conversely, no change in one renders no change in the other. Another way to put that might be, as the writer of Exodus seems to have done, that if we choose to see the world as our fathers did, we will live in the same world they did. Or, again, by deciding to employ the same perspective handed down to us on their knees by our parents (real and figurative) -- choose, as the saying goes, to be chips off the old block -- we are condemned to inheriting their world. Condemned not by an angry or unreasonable God meting out cruel punishment, but by ourselves for accepting the choices of others in a universe in which our choices determine our reality. Viewed in this way, the God who spoke to Moses here takes on the character not of a vengeful and insensitive judge unwilling to relieve us of the sins of our forebears, in whose guilt we could have had no part, but of a concerned Creator-Father explaining the way of things: see the universe as your fathers did, and yours shall be like theirs; see it as I do, as it is, and you can be freed of their misery. The same passage continues by observing that only the guilty, those who hate God (which we can understand to mean those who ignore or turn away from this lesson) are condemned; and those who love God (who seek to understand, accept, and adopt this principle) will be forgiven, or made free.

Let us pause here just a moment to develop another illustration-device in an effort to clarify this essential point, for we absolutely must get a firm grasp on it if we are to understand and integrate into our lives the rest.

A paradigm is a model or a pattern, sort of like the preset design chosen by a seamstress against which she cuts and shapes a bolt of cloth. And for our purposes in this inquiry, we can say that a paradigm is a way of looking at the universe: the mindset or mental surround that determines our perspective, indeed that *is* our perspective -- the preset design chosen by us against which we cut and shape our reality. Accordingly, everything we experience -- every thought and idea; each action we take and all the actions of others; the events near and far however much, directly or indirectly, they may seem relevant to us; our understanding of how things are and how they might be; all this and everything else -- comes to our awareness and is interpreted by us through the lens which is our paradigm. Clearly, then, we are talking here not just of a few biases, prejudices, and misconceptions (although at base it may amount to no more than that) but of the whole conceptual inheritance of humanity. Everything that any man ever said or did, or is saying or doing, in some way affects what we, you and I, say and do today -- so long, that is, as we accept the paradigms of our fathers and of their fathers (and, of course, mothers).

Consider a newborn child. He enters the world with a clean slate, into an arena whose rules and dimensions he knows nothing about, unaware even that he is a he and that the remainder is the arena. We should note that we are talking of a theoretical child and not a "real" baby, for the psychologists tell us now that adult patterns are set even in the womb and that the slate is far from clean at parturition. Almost as soon as he opens his eyes, this newly born child of ours is told how to see and what to believe, and so he does, until the slate is full and the paradigm set. Then he looks about him and sees the same world his parents did, a universe of competing elements of which he is just one part, threatened like the rest with hunger, disease, insecurity, and dissatisfaction of almost infinite variety (parental, marital, familial, sexual, vocational, governmental, environmental, and so on). To be sure, he will have some fun and good times along the way, but always lurking in the shadows will be reminders of his fragility -- the fragility of life being the cornerstone of his inherited paradigm.

But what if, in the first moments of life, our

theoretical child was blessed with an empty hospital room, and what if, in that silence, he heard not the voice of his mommy urging that he grow up to be like his daddy, but instead the voice of God which Moses heard reminding him that he need not be what others tell him he is. What then? Is it not possible that we are being urged to seek just such an empty surgery for ourselves by the New Testament teacher's lesson that unless we become like children we cannot be saved? It is not the foolish carelessness and blind naivete of a child that is salvation, surely he is telling us, but the abandonment of all the baggage of adulthood, the paradigms of our fathers, for it is these in a plutonic universe that imprison us. And it is in this light too that we can find one application of the otherwise disconcerting and inconsistent lesson that the truth will set a man against his father and a daughter against her mother, and that we must hate (turn away from) not only our families but our life itself -- as they taught us, and we have agreed, to see it. And, finally, this is the sense in which we might understand the concept of being born anew, of the virgin birth itself.

The New Testament tells us that the teacher was born of a virgin mother and was conceived by a divine act, and it is no mere coincidence that the lives of others of the world's most inspired and inspiring teachers are said to have begun in much the same way. If these reports are as much parable as history, as I suspect they might be, then the account of the teacher's virgin birth can be understood to be describing too a spiritual event which we as seekers must experience also. The new child within us, born in that empty surgery and fathered by an inner yearning to see whose source we cannot quite identify, is the beginning, marks the first genuine and irreversible step on our long journey forward. Recall, for a moment, the first youngster we spoke of in these pages, frustrated and frightened in his darkened bedroom. At some unpredictable instant, sparked perhaps by an indistinct and hardly tangible memory (or reminder, from some unseen past or by divine intervention) of how the room was, suppose he decided to begin looking for the light switch. By that act, born within him but prompted perhaps by something beyond, he is changed; to be sure, he is still scared and groping, but no longer is he sitting quivering on a corner of his bed, reacting fearfully to each rush of wind through a window or shifting shadow against the wall. Rather than just accepting the menacing dark as his inevitable fate or even simply screaming aloud for help, he has set out to understand the true nature of his reality, and to change it, for himself. Our challenge is exactly like his, and so is our promise. The divine germ of a new life is always within us, thank God, but it is we who must mother it to fruition, and the moment we will choose, or be prompted, to do so is as impossible to predict as the moment of the child's resolve to find the light. But at some point somewhere, sometime, we too will decide that we have had enough of life as it has been painted for us and that we want out badly enough that we are willing ourselves to find the way, to seek.

So we cannot but come to recognize that the only way out of this world, out of the misery, frustration, and competition which we find wherever we are on the ladder to so-called success, is to reject as our own its values; for so long as we accept as reality the refraction in the prism it will seem real to us. Herein is the essence of the New Testament's teachings, and our own findings about the plutonic nature of the universe are confirmed by it. Numerous times the teacher asserts (and in virtually the same words so do others who have seen as he did) that only those who believe in him will be saved, and however else we may choose to interpret that assertion, it can be seen as saying what we have already observed. For it seems extremely unlikely to me that he intended it as a threat, neither as an attempt to build an empire based on his person, as that was not the nature of this man. Rather, this was a tautology, an equation in which the two sides are equal to each other: unless we see as he did -- not believe in him as a separate, distinct individual, but believe in the validity of his vision -- we cannot be freed. This is a bit like saying that unless the sun has risen, there is no daylight, and when it has, there is. The one *is* the other. Seeing the universe as this man did, believing in him, is to become as he was, free of this world, because as we see, we are. *I am the way;* not the man but his teachings, not the flesh but the vision.

The Rich Man's Plight

So, we have seen that the concept of rebirth, of becoming like children, is to be taken nearly literally. It is not just a question of restructuring our ambitions within an already existing framework, of placing a bit more emphasis on piety, if you will, and a little less on the rest; we must instead start over altogether from scratch. And it is not an easy process (as any woman who has given birth can attest). Our New Testament teacher knew that, as he too had been where we are, and it was from a recognition of the enormity of the task before us that he likened our undertaking to the passage of a camel through the eye of a needle; for each of us is the rich man in that story who pleaded for an easy way.

In this world, wealth is measured by the accumulation of things. Money, of course, is representative of wealth, but it is not wealth itself for money has no intrinsic value of its own; its only worth lies in the extent to which it can be translated into things -- goods (look at that word and what it says about us!), services, and whatever else we crave. The popular conception of a rich man, then, is a person who wants and has lots of things; a poor man is one who wants them but does not have them. However, along the journey to the other side of the prism, so to speak, a rich man is one who has begun to see the truth of reality, and a poor man one who has not. It is from both of these perspectives on wealth that we must read the teacher's lesson in the story of the rich man urged to sell all he had and give to the poor. The teacher's intent could not have been simply that a man rich in a this-world sense liquidate his holdings and give the earnings to those without, however charitable an act that might be, because in the greater sense neither would benefit: the rich man would still want what he had given up, and would presumably instantly set out to amass again a fortune, and the poor would merely have added to their previously meager accumulation. A simple game of musical chairs that is, and not sufficient to the spiritual needs to which the teacher's lesson is addressed. On this journey, it is quite irrelevant whether or not we *have* things; what matters is whether or not we *want* them. So, when the rich man is urged in the story to sell all he has, we are all being told that the way to heaven -- to seeing aright -- is by abandoning our current standards of wealth, our old values, our fathers' paradigms. Only by that can we become truly rich (it not being sufficient, you will remember the teacher told the same man, just to *obey* his religion's commandments, simply to put more emphasis on piety). And when we truly have taken that essential step toward freeing ourselves from our own imprisonment, then and only then are we able to give to the poor -- that is, assist others who have not done so by alerting to their attention the true nature of their poverty. The teacher concluded and summarized this lesson quite logically with a beautifully gentle invitation -- and, incidentally, nowhere does he suggest forced acquiescence -- that we follow him, meaning that by turning away from the values of this world and helping others to do the same, we will go where, and as, he went, and see as he saw. Once again, the one is the other.

This identical lesson appears in the New Testament over and over again. To be sure, it is often addressed differently and offered in different contexts, but always the message is the same: to get on the proper track, we have to start over, from square one. None of the values of this world, none of our old paradigms, can we retain, for all of them are predicated on the refracted image of Truth that we see in the prism and out of which we have created a reality that is simply inaccurate, misleading, and inherently frustrating. And so long as we accept any of these old values as real, we accept as real the false premise on which all of them are based; we accept as real what we think we see in the glass, and it isn't. With the values of this world, we are forever blinded to reality as it is; with a vision, even a glimpse, of Truth, we can be freed. Or, in the teacher's words, with men (a this-world perspective) salvation is impossible; with God (Truth) all things are possible.

By Your Faith

The personal responsibility each of us bears in initiating, permitting, and fulfilling our own rebirthing process is perhaps nowhere better affirmed than in the numerous accounts of healing in the New Testament. There is ample evidence in many of these passages that their purpose is primarily to illustrate the lesson that to change ourselves we have to change our belief structures. No one can do it for us because no one can see for us, and as we see, we are. Too often are we prone to interpret these accounts of healings simply in terms of one man performing a miraculous action upon another, and then to revere the former accordingly. But the teacher was aware of that danger, and repeatedly he called our attention to it by reminding the healed that it was not he, the teacher, who was at work but their own faith.

Faith is a concept difficult to define and, if you haven't been there, virtually impossible to understand. Ordinarily, we think of faith as belief in something without any evidence to support it, and accordingly, we relegate faith to idealists and fools. But for our purposes in this discussion of the spiritual search, that definition of faith will not do because if what we find to be true about the nature of the universe is not supported by the world we see around us, and does not explain that world for us, then what we have seen is not truth and is of little use to us. Remember that we said that a measure of truth is that it must be true wherever applied. Or, again, if what we see, or are beginning to see, on the other side of the prism is not evidenced on this side as well (albeit in a refracted way), then we are still not seeing either correctly, for they are at base the same thing -- the one is the other. In this sense, faith about Heaven (Truth) is not pie-in-the-sky stuff, but conviction based upon understanding. Faith then is knowledge -- not the ordinary, "book learning" knowledge of this world, but an awareness, realization, and application of the meaning of the plutonic nature of reality and of the prism effect construction. Faith is knowledge which can be and is supported by the evidence of this world when we begin looking at it properly. Faith is never blind; indeed, faith is vision, corrected sight.

In any conversation of a serious subject, it is quickly apparent whether the speaker truly sees what he is saying or whether he is groping about in the dark, repeating what he has heard from others, even just making noise. Throughout the New Testament there are many reports that the teacher, apparently unlike some other religious leaders of his time, spoke with authority. What he said he knew to be true for he had seen it. That is what is meant in this inquiry by faith, and anything less is something else.

By our faith are we healed, and as its root suggests, that verb means to be made whole. In a universe keyed to our choices about it, if we wish to be made whole, to see ourselves as we are, not separate but One, then we must choose to reject the choices we have lived by until now and select instead the one that is the One, elect to seek and live the kind of knowledge we have spoken of as faith. If we will examine the healing accounts in their parable sense, we can find in the characters and their conditions aspects of ourselves along the path: the teacher as healer is Truth which resides within us, and the infirm our current state. It is no mere coincidence that the latter are portrayed as crippled, blind, disfigured, or even dead, all symbols of our inability to function properly in a universe seen wrong. And the reaching for the healing touch is the inner act by which we first reach for wholeness. In most, if not all, of the accounts, it is the sick who seek out the teacher, just as it is we who must initiate our search. And when the teacher said, as he did, to those he touched that it was their faith that healed them, we must understand that it is our re-awakening to Truth that renders us whole. Perhaps the account most illustrative of this interpretation is the one about the centurion who asked for help for a servant sick at home, and who said, when the teacher offered to go to the house, that it would be enough if he would just say the word, that he knew the man would then be healed. Here is faith as we have described it personified. The choice for Truth affects and changes everything in our lives, and when we see it anywhere, we see it everywhere.

All of what we have said in this brief examination of healing is true in a literal sense as well as the parable one we addressed. Faith healing can be an effective method of dealing with disease, and successful cases of it are known to most of us. And those involved with this practice generally agree that the degree and duration of success are directly a factor of the patient's confidence in the process, of his expectations of what will, what can, happen. In effect, the patient in these cases heals himself, by letting go the conviction that his illness is inevitable and adopting instead the possibility of wholeness.

The healer simply assists, like a midwife at a birthing. By accepting the healer's version of reality --that he can heal the sick -- the patient makes a new choice for his own reality, and the universe being plutonic, if the choice is certain, it works. What is true as parable is equally true as literal, for, once again, the truth is true everywhere and at every level of application.

Finally, as the word itself suggests, the "rebirth" is just the beginning, and the newborn infant within us who has just barely opened his eyes to the light will require much attention, nutrition, guidance, reinforcement, discipline, and fondling -- all the mothering of his literal counterpart. He should be exposed only carefully and gradually to inclement weather and to other external influences; and, until ready to stand on his own, he should be shielded from rowdies, bullies, know-it-alls, and their like. Once begun, this spiritual process is virtually irreversible, but there are hazards ahead which can delay, complicate, confuse, and misdirect it, and until we have a grasp on it, we do well to lay low. Quite understandably, most of us in a burst of initial enthusiasm over this momentous event are moved to shout it from the rooftops and to pass out cigars, as it were, to all and sundry. But we must restrain that impulse, for others are not likely to rejoice at the event as we do, seeing it instead as a threat to themselves and their values -- the very abandonment of which, we are reminded, being what made possible the rebirth in the first instance. Rather than sharing our jubilation, they will try to dampen, even extinguish, it. Mindful of this danger, the New Testament teacher warned the newly healed to be silent about it, to say nothing to anyone, not to make known to others what has occurred within us. Like the newborn of any species, we are yet fragile, and can be too easily persuaded back to our old ways of seeing by the pressure, disbelief, and ridicule of others. Although we have changed, to be sure, we are too still much the same, for a mere glimpse of knowledge is not enough to erase ignorance. And inevitably we will succumb from time to time to seeing again as we have been used to, to forgetting the reality of Truth and acknowledging the truth of error.

Two Gospel accounts, if we will look at them as parables for a moment, speak to this very normal tendency to waiver. In the first, the teacher and his disciples are described as being in a boat beset by a storm at sea; in fear for their lives, the disciples call out to him for rescue. We are told that the teacher is asleep at the time, and if we can understand him here to be representing the newly reborn knowledge of Truth within us, the lesson of the story becomes apparent. Likewise, in the second example, again set in a boat, one of the disciples is encouraged by the teacher to walk on the water as he himself had done, but, although successful at first, the disciple begins to sink when distracted and frightened by the wind and waves, the commotion, around him. In both cases, the teacher said it was the disciple's too little faith that brought failure; when awake and alert, we see, but when lulled again into sleep or distracted by the familiar old ways around us, we stumble. It is the Truth that makes us free, as he said, but the extent of our freedom depends directly on the depth, certainty, and constancy of our faith. To be free we must acknowledge the Truth, we must *know* it so thoroughly and constantly that it becomes us, and only so much as we do, does it. If what we see we are, then clearly if we want to be the Truth, we must not let our eyes stray from it. Or, again in his words, according to our faith is it done. And total faith (all pervasive, ever-present knowledge of Truth) requires time, effort, commitment, silence, and care, for healthy,full, and effective growth. Having made the choice for it, we must also make the choice to nurture it. Like the motherhood of the literal kind this is no mean enterprise.

Of Fruit And Fruits

We live in a world, perhaps especially in the technologically industrialized West, governed by experts, and few of us make decisions without turning consciously or unconsciously to one or another of them for their opinions, advice, encouragement, or direction. From matters of health and finance to the selection of a brand of toothpaste, we permit our affairs to be guided, even determined, by others, most of whom earn their position of authority by little else than our own acquiescence. As the physicists tell us, nature abhors a vacuum, and if we will not take charge of ourselves, someone else will. If only from habit alone, we are equally prone to look to others as we set out on the spiritual search. And others will be there, anxious for followers. The problem here is that, while allowing a rock-star to select a deoderant for us may seem harmless enough, permitting another to dictate our choices along the spiritual way is an abdication of personal responsibility fraught with risks. This is not to suggest that we cannot benefit from the experience of others, or that we cannot learn from them, for we can. But learning is one thing; blind and thoughtless acquiescence is quite another.

The New Testament teacher was alert to the tendency among men to surrender their destinies to others, and he repeatedly warned us against it. There will be many, he said, and how right he was!, who will posture themselves as worthy of our devotion and allegiance; but we can know them, he taught, suggesting to us the best possible measure of a man, by their fruits. When one comes before us offering himself as our salvation, we should look not to his physical appearance, surface trappings, or apparent spirituality, but at his words and works, his actions and direction, and at those who have chosen to follow him. These are a teacher's fruits, and while they may be sweet to others, if they fail to speak to that inner yearning within us not for the security of abject surrender but for knowledge at whatever cost or difficulty, then we may find them a bitter harvest. And remember too that a teacher's disciple - become -teacher, whatever he may say or think about himself, cannot speak for anyone but himself. Too many would have us hear from their lips another's voice, but just as we can see only for ourselves based upon who and what we are inside, so it is with speaking. Every teacher speaks for himself alone and only as he himself sees the universe, whatever his training, references, and bibliography. We might be reminded here of the parable about the son who, when instructed by his father to work in the family vineyard, agreed to do so but then did not. Likewise, there are inevitably some among us who profess to be working in the vineyard, perhaps even honestly think themselves to be doing so, but are not. Their focus is not on what lies beyond the prism, not on the One, and the thrust of their teaching is not to call attention to the distortion effect of the glass; instead, they seek to convince us merely to substitute one erroneous interpretation of the refraction for another. New wine in old skins, and we can recognize the containers for what they are, whatever their fancy packaging and alluring labels, if we will remain alert to the taste of the wine that pours forth from them. Does it smack of all the old assumptions and values, however well disguised? Has a new piece of cloth, to change metaphors, simply been sewn onto an old bolt following the familiar pattern? Are we in short being urged to see the world as we always have -- as separate, hostile, threatening, and impermanent -- except in different language? We can know a tree by its fruit, and if we seem simply to be swapping apples for pears, we are likely in the same orchard we grew up in, and should move on. There is only one true vine, Truth, and while it may be known by various names and grow in a variety of shapes, its fruit is forever the same, vision. That is the fruit we seek, and we will know when we have found it.

If we must be so careful in our selection of guides and if, as we will, we need direction from time to time, where are we to turn? In a word, inward. Go into a closet, the teacher said, for it is there, not in the streets, that we can find true guidance. Behind the closed doors of our private sanctuary, away from the chatter and static of the world, there yet burns a light, if now only faintly, which will illuminate the path for us. In that surgery, empty of meddling and distractions, we will hear a voice which speaks of our rebirth and will deliver us through it. If this seems a lonely solution, it is because loneliness is of the separate and separative world we are used to. In the within we are in the company of the One, and there loneliness is unknown, for there we come to see that the One and we are one, there being nothing else. And it is there that we can and must surrender; not to another, however, but to ourselves, to the Truth within, and that is, us -- to the One that is God. We surrender the stubborn and crystallizing self-assurance which we have developed to protect us from our perceived competitors and predators without, to the quiet and releasing mystery of the new way. This surrender is not abdication of authority but assumption of responsibility, and it will seem, as it is, perfectly natural. And in our outer lives, our initial loneliness too will quickly vanish as we seek the company of, and are joined by, others along the same path. As like attracts like, this is a process which we should not force or hurry, but simply allow to happen, always mindful of the difference between fruit and fruits.

On Sin And The Forgiveness Of Sins

Already we have said a good deal, if indirectly, about sin, and by now our conception of it should be changed considerably. But still sin is an idea so integral to our culture and one so thoroughly misunderstood with such frightening and disturbing consequences, that specific attention to it, even at the risk of some repetition, is warranted. To put it as simply as possible, if The Fall (which some traditions refer to as Original Sin) can be represented as the choice to see the One as fragmented, to accept as real and as all there is our confusion about the image in the prism, then sin is nothing more, or less, than the choice not to question that first choice for error and indeed to continue in it. Sin is the choice to see wrongly. And the punishment for sin is its consequence: the world and life as we know it now -- fragile, insecure, unsatisfying, senseless, and erratic.

God does not judge our sins, and neither does he punish us for them, for we are told that He sees us as we truly are, as in His image, and thus as incapable of sin, or error. After all, only those, us, who see incorrectly see incorrectly! When we choose to see the One erroneously, we do not change its nature, and those aspects of the One which have not made that choice for error continue to be, and see, as before. Or, again, when we choose to stand on this side of the prism and then describe the One seen through it as many, that which is on the other side does not and cannot see what we see, because it is not looking at itself or us through the prism as we are doing. Our error, then, is not transferable, and it is an intergral part of the error to assume, as we do, that God too is subject to it, that He can see it. As complicated as this reasoning may seem, it is crucial that we get a grasp on it in order to free ourselves of the crippling fear of sin and of a vindictive, judgemental Divinity. God seems that way to us now because we see Him as separate from us (as we see everything else), as standing apart or above, looking down, meting out punishment and reward to His subjects. Again, He seems that way to us and to be doing those things to us because we view Him and our lives from a this-side-of-the-prism perspective. That is not the case, of course, precisely because He does not see us as separate from Him as in Truth we are not. To recall again an earlier illustration, the parents of the child in his darkened bedroom do not see the dragons not because they, the parents, are insensitive or blind but because they see the room as it actually is and always has been, beast-free. You are mistaken, they will say comfortingly to the boy, as God says to us, for you are seeing what is there altogether incorrectly, and to see as I do, you have only to turn on the light. No punishment, just loving advice.

In at least one currently available version of the New Testament, the word sin is footnoted as being from the Greek for stumbling block, and if we portray the reach for Truth as a path we travel, as we here and others have done, we can see how appropriate a word that is. As we trip and fall over the obstacles in our way, inevitably is our attention distracted from the destination, and our pace slowed. But anyone who has gone through a forest with an accomplished woodsman has seen how the latter walks differently than he might on an urban sidewalk. Here in the woods, the professional is always alert to fallen trees, protruding roots, and moss - covered rocks. His pace is measured, his steps sure, and his attention keenly focused on the landmarks around and ahead of him. We too, in setting out on this path, must abandon our old ways of tredding, our city habits, for what is appropriate in that world will cause us to stumble in this new one. Thus, the teacher urges us to cut off the limb or pluck out the eye which causes us to stumble, to abandon the values, habits, and perspective which are our stumbling blocks.

If God does not judge and forgive sins, then who does? We ourselves. But only our own. And we do so by recognizing, in the first instance, that we have chosen to see wrongly, and, then, in the second, by determining to correct that error. We cannot forgive others, of course, because the very act of seeing them *as* others is an aspect of our own sin, of our initial and continuing choice to see the world and them as it and they are not. To the extent that we can forgive them, it is by finally seeing them as they are, one with us, one with the One, but our action then is internal, not external. And from all this it follows that no sins are greater than any others. In a world seen as separate and many, we think of our actions in the same way, but to suggest that there are degrees and kinds of sins is to miss the point entirely. Incorrect vision is incorrect vision, however often or differently it may seem to manifest. Whether we stumble over a pebble or a boulder, we stumble nonetheless, and it is not the pebble or the boulder which is the sin so much as it is the stumbling, the failure to see the obstacle for what it is, and to step over it. The woodsman, in those rare instances when he trips, does not curse the offending log (well, he ought not) but his own inattention, for he knows that only the ever alert pathfinder makes it to the other side.

Those familiar with the New Testament will by now have recalled the warning that of all possible sins there is one that is unforgivable, to wit blasphemy of, or speaking against, the Holy Spirit. We suggested earlier that God is not aware of our sins because He does not see as we are seeing, and yet, in a way we cannot understand, surely He is aware that an aspect of the One has somehow seemed to itself to have separated out from the whole, has chosen error. Recognizing that occurrence, but not acknowledging its reality, He would presumably create a corrective measure, and we might think, for a moment, of the Holy Spirit in that way. If we will imagine the Holy Spirit as the Teacher of Truth -- that is, as that characteristic or aspect of Truth which constantly tries to call our attention to itself and to our true selves (a cosmic burr in our saddle, if you like) -- we can see him, or it, if you prefer, as the one aspect of the One which is on this side of the prism and on the other side at the same time and knows it; and, further, acknowledges this side solely to alert us to our error. The Holy Spirit did not make the error we made and then seek to return to the Truth as we are doing. The Holy Spirit, we might say, came from Truth to re-awaken us to it but never himself lost sight of it, as we have done. He can see the error and the Truth, which he is, at the same time, and point out the difference to us. Again, a Cosmic Teacher, the Truth reasserting Truth. If this description is anywhere near the mark, it becomes apparent that the choice not to listen to the Holy Spirit's constant promptings, indeed to turn away from them, dooms us. It is the one choice which by definition keeps us in the dark eternally, or exactly as long as we opt for it -- that moment of choice, so long as we live by it, being all the time there is, or eternity. It is an unforgivable sin in precisely the sense that we cannot be forgiven of it until we for-give (give up or release) the mindset which led us to it. So long, in a word, as we are deaf to the Holy Spirit, we are blind to the Truth. Forever, if that's how long we choose deafness. As the New Testament teacher put it, we are either for him, meaning, surely, his teachings or his vision, or against him. We either look to Truth directly or we accept as true our mistaken interpretation of the refraction in the prism.

Viewed from this perspective, the connection between sin and death which is so often made in the New Testament becomes clear. So long as we choose to accept the illusory or distorted sense of reality handed down by our fathers -- that is, so long as we are determined to look away from Truth to error, or to sin -- that long are we destined to live in the world manifested by that choice, by that paradigm, a world in which death so obviously plays an essential part. Indeed, we might amend the scriptural teaching that the wages of sin is death, to read, the wages of sin are death and life, with a lower case L, because our lives as we know them now and our death are both a product of our choice for error. Confirming this interpretation is the teacher's assertion that a man need not die to see the Truth. Again, death is simply one aspect of this world, of Truth seen wrongly, and it assures us of nothing but itself. What follows death depends upon what each of us believes is its aftermath, for death too is an aspect of a universe which reflects our beliefs about it. Once again, the answer lies not in trying to make sense out of, or find comfort in, what we have chosen to see in the prism, but in recognizing the prism for what it is and choosing to discard it altogether. Only by opting for Truth do we begin to recognize its manifestations and eventually to see it and ourselves as the One we are.

Finally, we might examine in this same context the almost overpowering proclamation that no man may see the face of God and live, an idea often portrayed in films by a shuddering desert shepherd peeking sheepishly through his fingers at the source of some blinding light or thundering voice and being instantly turned to stone. To be sure, in a parable sense that image might be helpful in explaining this concept. But we can understand the assertion to be underlining what we have discovered -- that in order to see reality as it is we must abandon *all* our old ways of thought, our old paradigms, and turn literally right around, and in doing so are we totally changed. Thus, the man who sees God, who turns from error to Truth, ceases by that act to be the man he was, or better, believed he was. The "old" man dies, disappears, when the light is turned on, and a new one, the real One, is re-born. No man can see the Truth and live because what lives after the event is in no wise what lived before. We are changed by that "event"; not change within the old framework in which all change renders only more of the same, but changed in kind, resulting in none of the same. Or again, we become as unlike what we were as what we thought we were was unlike what we actually are. Viewed from this side of the prism, of course, none of that makes any sense, but then neither does anything viewed solely from this side of the prism.

A SECOND LOOK

Our inquiry through the preceding chapters has brought us to the conclusion that our lives in this world seem to be a direct, accurate, and immediate reflection of our beliefs about life. That is, our beliefs determine for us what we will see, hear, and experience at every level or point of our existence. Whatever we may think about the affect of external events in influencing the course of our lives, the fact seems to be that the determining action is all internal. Despite the appearances, we do not react to external events in the shaping of our lives so much as we use, shape, and initiate external events, however unconsciously, and choose from among them, and from various possible interpretations of them, to confirm and reinforce what we believe to be true and therefore expect to occur. We see, hear, and experience what we expect to see, hear, and experience, and that is determined by our beliefs. Indeed, what seems to occur externally and independently of us, at least as we see those occurrences, may actually be no more than, but all of, an outer manifestation of what we are within.

In the first sentence above we might have used both the lower and the upper cases for the word life, so that it would have read, our lives in this world are a reflection of our beliefs about life and about Life. The former indicating our activities in the day-to-day, so-called real world, or ordinary life as we see it, and the latter Creation or the Universe as it is seen by God or the Creator, as it really is. The first we might think of as earth, the second as heaven; but the problem with those words used that way, or rather with the way we generally interpret them, is that we tend to think of them as referring to two different places. Earth is here, heaven out there somewhere, but as we have suggested, the difference is much more one of understanding or awareness than it is of location. To use the terms we have developed in this book, the former, life, might represent the confused conclusion and erroneous framework we have developed from the image in the prism, and the latter, Life, the One or Truth beyond the glass. Ordinarily, as I have said, we tend to think of these two as being virtually unrelated, certainly at least very different in nature and quality -- the one is here, the other somewhere else -- but as our prism effect model indicated, and is intended to indicate, they really are one and the same, except looked at differently. Thus, although what we see in the prism is a refraction of the light beyond it, it is nonetheless the light itself. And so, what we -- at the Fall --

originally saw in the prism may not have been so erroneous as it was potentially highly misleading, a potentiality which we actualized by proceeding from that point to the unfortunate next in which we "forgot" the source of the prism's image and built an understanding of the universe on that mistake. Remember that we said earlier in our scenario for The Fall that what may have happened "in the beginning" after one aspect or element of the One somehow for some unknowable reason saw itself and the Whole of which it was, and is, a part, as not One, but many, is that this miscreant forgot, in fascination at its dubious achievement, what it had done and came to accept the refracted image as all there was and as fully complete; and, worse yet, from there we said it may have developed an ever complicating set of erroneous interpretations of what it thought it was seeing, and then taught its offspring to see the image in the same wrong way. Thus, what we experience in, around, and as ourselves is the One but seen all wrong. Now, if that is what happened, or nearly what happened, then to erase the error, or to cancel The Fall by rising again, we must seek to reverse the process, and we may be able to do that by undertaking to rid ourselves of the delusionary and confusing interpretations and explanations of reality which we have inherited over the ages since that first rascal did his dirty deed.

The Lion And The Lamb

Unfortunately, when we come to realize that all these years we have, in effect, been had, that the old values, standards, and perspectives lead nowhere and produce nothing but more of themselves, we are initially moved, both from enthusiasm and resentment, to reject and abandon not only the inaccurate yardsticks but the world itself. At our first exposure to, or re-encounter with, Truth, we want to turn to it totally, as indeed we must, and often we understand that to mean turning our back on or shutting our eyes to everything else. This sentiment is normal but mistaken, and, if not encouraged, it will dissipate of its own accord. Let it do so. For the fact is that we cannot hide from the world outside us and neither should we want to, any more than we can hide from ourselves, for the two are, as we have seen, one and the same. Wherever we go, we take our outside world with us, like a shadow -- actually, very much like a shadow. However romantic the promise of physical isolation may seem, there exists no mountain cave where if we are there, our world is not there too. To be sure, there is merit in seeking solitude from time to time, there to conduct the inner search without distraction or interruptions. As with the total immersion method of teaching foreign languages, this approach can facilitate rapid and effective change, but if inner change has been wrought, then it must be witnessed outside too, even in and about the cave, if that is the world we have chosen. As we come to understand this principle, we can begin to make good use of the world apparently outside us as an indicator of what is being accomplished within us. We can learn to recognize in the shadow the shape and nature of the thing which casts it, we ourselves. Thus, again, in a plutonic universe, what is outside comes from within, and just as the images on a movie screen are determined by the film in the projector and there is clearly no point to rejecting or destroying the screen to protest displeasing footage, so it is with our lives. It is to the film within the projector that change is necessary, and what we see on the screen can and should alert us to that need. Whatever we witness that seems to us ugly, distasteful, or in any sense disturbing, should flag to our attention those traits within us, for we cannot see what we do not project.

Similarly, when we react with anger toward others, regardless of the provocation and our claims of innocence in the exchange, we must recognize that there remains anger within, however much at inner peace we may feel. Fear and insecurity prompted by apparently entirely outside influences should speak to us of our unresolved inner fears and insecurity. And hunger and cravings of every kind can alert us to a lingering hunger within, however fully nourished spiritually we believe ourselves to be. So long, in a word, as we see the lion and the lamb of the world's jungle locked in bitter enmity, then so are they in our own, for it is the persistence of the latter which we see and abhor and have projected onto the former. Or, again, when we have beaten our inner swords into plowshares, then will we see the makings of plowshares in all swords, but until then we will not, nay we cannot -- for as we are within, so we see and so it is.

Remember that in the New Testament we are taught to love our neighbors as ourselves, and this not because to do so is nice, sociable behavior, although surely it is that, but precisely and literally because our neighbors as we see them *are* ourselves. Likewise, we are urged to love our enemies, or those we dislike, and this again because they are our mirrors: what we see in them that alienates us are the same ugly traits which still reside within us. Others can awaken within us only what is there, and where there is still anger, it must surface and be seen. Our enemies, by seeming to cause that anger to rise up -- seeming, because it is we who are projecting it, not they who are eliciting it -- do us a dear service, and one worthy of our love, for without them we might not be aware of that lingering trace.

Notice here that what seems to be significant is *how* we react to or interpret the events and experiences around us, the value we place on them.

Clearly, this raises the question, if it has not already come to mind, of whether or not there *is* an absolute reality "out there" which is neutral and which each of us interprets and labels in our own way according to who and where we are at the moment of observation. Certainly an elephant seen in a circus act for the first time by a city-bred child seems a very different phenomenon to him than the same species would appear to a professional zoologist at work in the African bush, and yet the beast before each may very well be the same animal. We may want to ask ourselves, is there actually an elephant out there, a thing which, while it may seem different to different viewers, has a reality of its own irrespective of what those looking at it may think about it? Unfortunately, while we cannot avoid dealing with this question sooner or later, I am not at all sure that there is any merit in our doing so now, because whatever may indeed be "out there" (something or no-thing), we now all of us act and react according to our perceived reality, that is, according to what we think we see out there and that is determined by what we think about it. My own guess is that once we finally see ourselves and our world as the One they truly are — that is, see through the confused and confusing interpretations of the image in the prism and beyond that to the Light Source itself -- the question will have resolved itself for we will no longer be the we that we think we are now and presumably neither will the elephant. But, for the moment, what we think we are seeing is all we can really be interested in (on the understanding that our reach, if not our grasp, exceeds that); in any event it is certainly all that we now seem to react to and live by. Consider for example a volcanic eruption: as an act of nature, it has no relative value. The wildlife overtaken by the lava flow and the landscape altered by it presumably make no judgment about it, and neither does a rainstorm consider itself the less by comparison. And yet we measure, label, categorize, and price it the instant we become aware of it, and each of us does so according to his own perceived stake or interest in it. A neighboring rancher may be distressed by his losses, a geologist excited by the prospect of new insights, and a sightseer enthralled by the awesome beauty. Each is witnessing the same event but would describe it in very different terms, and so for each, it would be an event almost entirely different from that observed by the others. In this connection, consider the fact that we always refer to such events as natural "disasters", measuring them as we do solely by their effect on the things we value! Similarly, almost any police officer will report that often there are as many differing versions of a civil disturbance as there were witnesses to it. The point seems to be that we do not experience reality in an impartial or neutral manner so much as we observe it through senses which are shaded, blinded, and tuned by our value systems, by our beliefs about who and what we are. Thus, a partial answer to the question we just agreed not to tangle with may lie in our tendency to equate awareness and perception, not recognizing that the first might be better understood as the process by which information comes to us and the latter as the way in which we interpret it. Because they now seem the same to us, we think of the two as occurring simultaneously, but if we can learn to separate them we may be able to acquire the ability of true awareness by which we simply experience reality without judging it or in any way measuring its impact on us. This effort may or may not help answer that thorny question, but it will I think facilitate our seeing our lives differently. Recall the squirrel we spoke of in a previous chapter where we said that we tend to think of him as building a cache of seeds and nuts as security against the winter ahead. Because we are frightened by the prospect of starvation, we assume that he is, and we transfer our fear to him and then interpret his actions accordingly. By our perception of life, as constantly threatened by insecurity, we interpret the squirrel's activities. But what we are seeing and describing in that instance is our own fear, not his, and his activities seem frantic to us precisely because we are frantic about the future. The problem may very well be that we are inclined to think of events as happening *to* us, as something against which we must have constantly prepared defenses, plans of action ready for instant implementation by which to deflect or neutralize what lies around the corner, and which we presume to be more than likely harmful to our interests. Perhaps if we can substitute this antagonistic view of reality with what we might call a participatory one, we may come closer to seeing things as they actually are.

On Bread, Wine, And Pancake Syrup

One of the techniques we can usefully employ in an effort to shift our view of reality from an antagonistic to a participatory one may be found in learning to see the events in our lives less as isolated and unrelated incidents involving us as performers and other persons or things as products, and more as whole processes in which we are but a partial or contributing element. Consider, for instance, the process "mapling", a term used in some parts of this country to describe the collection and preparation of maple tree sap for sweet syrup. Required in this annual undertaking are the sugar maples themselves, of course, but also the right combination of warm days and cold nights at the proper time of year, a drill and bit, taps, buckets, a fire and the appropriate pot for boiling, and a person, to name just a few of the ingredients. All of these are distinct and identifiable elements as we see them now, but for mapling to occur each of them must be present, and if any one is absent, there is no mapling. Each then has a role to play, none of which is, in a true analysis, more or less important than another. Now, we tend to think of ourselves as the catalysts in the equation, the element which makes it all happen, but might we not also be able to suggest that perhaps it is that, at just the correct moment, when each of the necessary elements has reached what we might call the state of mapling-ness, they gather together to become the process mapling. Or again, consider dining: instead of seeing this common daily practice as consisting of a person (subject) eating (verb) food (object) we might look at it as a process in which several elements are involved and by which each is changed. The process itself then becomes both the subject and the verb, and there is no object; dining simply occurs. It is something which happens, a happening. As we get to feel more comfortable viewing simple activities in this way, we can extend the horizons into space and time to encompass related activities. For example, the process mapling might be expanded to include the initial tree planting, acquisition and use of the materials to cut a path through the woods, the manufacture and sale of the drill and bit, and, when we are ready to go this far, even our own birth. What happens as we take on this altered way of seeing is that the concepts of space and time as we had known them begin to get a little fuzzy around the edges while a sense of the inter-connectedness (dare we say unity?) of things starts to develop within us, tentatively and intermittently at first, but with increasing certainty, regularity, and even, finally, constancy.

Learning to see our individual activities and then even our entire lives as complete processes rather than as distinct events comprised of separate subject-verb-object combinations requires something like the visual shift in perspective experienced in an optical illusion in which, for example, a set of straight lines on a flat page can be viewed as a box coming toward or receding from the observer. To effect the shift, we have to blink inwardly, as it were, and look again. Sometimes it will work, usually initially when we least expect it, and at others it will not, but if we persevere in our determination the shift will happen. Remember, our beliefs about the universe determine its reality for us, so as we begin to entertain new beliefs about it, however weakly and experimentally at first, we must come to see it accordingly. The old saying -- if wishes were horses, beggars would ride -- has application here in what we might call the beggar's horse effect:

by wanting to change our lives, to abandon the old paradigms and adopt new perspectives leading to direct vision of the truth, we will find that we will begin to do so, to see differently. Again, just for an isolated instant or two at first, but as we continue to affirm the desire and strengthen the will, ever reinforcing our determination to succeed, the instants will become moments, and then series of moments, all as the foundations of our old structure crumbles from lack of attention and the new framework takes shape. Fortunately, inertia works both ways: it may be hard to get the old underway, but once we do, it tends to want to continue moving. To be sure, wanting to effect this change is not by itself enough, and nothing here is intended to suggest that, but the will to do it is an essential and promiseful first step. Once the beggar has the horse, of course, he must learn to ride and know the direction he wants to take.

At an event we have come to call the Last Supper, the New Testament teacher spoke to his disciples in terms similar to our own here by urging those at the table to think of the bread as his body and the wine as his blood. In these few words, whose interpretation has been legion and each of which has its own merit, he seems to me to have captured the essence of his teaching: what is outside is inside; the two are inseparable, for each is the other, one and the same. The universe is plutonic. Once again using an experience familiar to all men -- and it could not have been an accident that he chose items so ordinary, common, and routine as bread and wine; the very staples of daily life here selected to serve as an illustration of the nature of Life itself -- the teacher reminds us that when we eat and drink we should not think of the food as things separate from us, or as separate from him, things grown, harvested, and produced by other separate persons in places distant and apart from us, for thinking in that way is to continue to live by the illusions of our fathers. Instead, we should see in the bread and in the wine, and in the process that put them on our table, a manifestation of ourselves, of our own bodies and blood, of what we believe ourselves and reality to be. Only if we try to see the bread and the wine *and* everthing, else in this expanded and en-*light*-ened way will we begin to understand what he meant and come to see as he saw. And we must seek to do so not just once a week or in special ceremonies, but always -- or at least as often, say, as we eat, which activity we never seem too busy to fit into our schedules! If we are to see the One and to know that we are a part of and in the One, then we must realize that we can see no-thing else, for there is nothing else: what is One *is* one. This is not just a cerebral exercise or a game for theorists; it is practical stuff to be dealt with right now, right here, at the dinner table. We, and the bread, and the wine, and the process by which all three came together, are one, One, and that is the Truth -- being at one with the Universe, or at-one-ment.

Who Do You Say I Am?

In the New Testament, the teacher is reported to have asked his disciples a question which we can interpret here to have been another application of this same, now familiar principle that in order to change our sense of the universe we must alter our way of seeing it. The question was, quite simply, "who do you say I am?" It seems an innocent enough question on its face, but look again, for it's loaded. As the teacher certainly recognized, however we answer that will instantly and unmistakably reveal where we are along the way toward fully integrating into our consciousness his teachings about the true nature of the universe, of reality, and of ourselves. If our answer centers around the teacher's apparent personality and performance, his this-wordliness in any of its religious, political, or social manifestations and ramifications, we show ourselves to be still thinking in the terms of this world, still bound by the limitations of our fathers' paradigms; we will have seen the teacher as a separate individual come amongst us to alter, if improve upon, reality within our accepted existing framework -- new wine in old skins. On the other hand, if our reply is focused beyond this world, on the truth of the teachings and not the mortal-ness of the teacher, on what lies beyond the prism and not on what we think we see in it, then we will have demonstrated that we have begun to shed the inherited and chosen perceptions which heretofore we have confused with, and acknowledged as, vision. To be sure, this latter answer cannot really be put into words, being beyond the capacity of language to communicate and reflecting more a state of being than an idea or concept to be expounded, but the teacher and others with true vision -- with ears to hear, as he puts it -- will understand, will see, what the inadequate words are meant to convey. Many spiritual traditions employ these kinds of questions between a teacher and his students, and there is no "right" answer to them in the sense that there is to an academic or professional examination, for these are intended more as probes into a seeker's consciousness, rattles to awaken the sleeping awareness of Truth within. Likewise, because the question is more an experience than a test, it is not enough for us simply to repeat another's answer which was seen to elicit a favorable reaction from the teacher. Unless we *see* as that other did, we cannot answer as he did, even though we think we are doing so by voicing his words. Not knowing as he knows or seeing as he sees, we can only interpret his answer within the limits of our own understanding and fall short, as it falls short.

A corollary to the principle resident in the question, who do you say I am?, might be stated, I am who you say I am. That is, what we see in and think of another is determined by what we believe about the nature of individual personality, of life, of reality itself, and thus any person we address will appear to us as he does because of who and what we believe ourselves to be, through and by which belief we perceive, measure, and categorize others. This is most emphatically not to say that we are for ourselves what others think of us, but we are so for them. Thus, the teacher is reported to have responded in effect to his accusers that he was who they said he was *if they said so*. Having chosen to see him through their existing belief structure which labelled the likes of him traitor, blasphemer, and a threat to order, they could not see him as otherwise, and so, from their point of view, so he was. No amount of verbal argument or emotional persuasion on his part could change their belief structure. Like them, we too are deaf and blind to all except that which confirms or reinforces our existing beliefs because it is those through and by which we accept, screen, and interpret everything we experience. We cannot conceive of what we do not believe is possible. To see differently, and thus to know and become the right answer to the teacher's question -- which, incidentally, we can direct to anyone or anything, including ourselves, as in: who or what do I say that thing is, or I am? -- we must change ourselves, and we do that by altering our belief or value structure.

Put Not Asunder What Is Joined

We have seen that common, ordinary occurrences, phenomena, and relationships can be effectively employed to teach us something about the spiritual journey and our progress along it; indeed, in the final analysis, this may be their only real purpose. Because what is outer is inner, we can and should use the world around us and our feelings about it as a curriculum for the study of ourselves and of our true nature. The new Testament teacher, as should be clear by now, was a master at this technique, and perhaps nowhere is his skill better evidenced than in his lesson on marriage and divorce. Here is an issue which confronts many of us, either directly or indirectly, and when it does, it tends to be in a highly personal, emotion-charged context. The teacher asks us to step back, however, and look at this aspect of human life as an illustration of Universal Truth, and from it to draw application for our own lives.

In the incident, the teacher was asked if there were any just cause for a man to leave his wife. He responded that from the beginning God had made them male and female and that it was for this reason that a man leaves his parents to be joined to a wife, the two becoming one flesh. He concluded that what God had joined, man should not put asunder. In our predictable hassling over a liberal or conservative literal interpretation of this story, endlessly looking for loopholes to accomodate our immediate, this-world desires, we may have missed the essential underlying point altogether, which is: by seeing the One as many, through the prism, and by creating our own separative sense of reality from that refraction, we have put asunder what is joined, seen as separate and separated what is neither. The sanctity of marriage as such, then, is not the central issue here, and the lesson is therefore intended to be as relevant to those among us who are not married as to those who are.

The teacher's observation that from the beginning God made the couple male and female will call to mind, for those who have studied it, the Eastern traditon that all life, and Life, has two aspects: yin and yang, passive and active, negative and positive, female and male, to mention only some of the labels employed. Never are these two seen as separate and distinct entities, but rather as alternating or complementary characteristics of one whole, like two sides of a coin. Neither is complete or even possible without the other, just as the tails side of a coin cannot exist without the heads. The two, then, are not connected or attached, but simply different aspects of the same thing. And when they are not in balance, when one is emphasized at the expense of the other, when, in ignorance of their nature, separation of the two is attempted, it is the whole which suffers. It is to precisely this concept that the teacher is pointing in this lesson. In the institution of marriage in our outer lives he would have us see a manifestation of the inner process he urges upon us. We have, he said, been created with, or as, two aspects, male and female, and it is the natural order of things for these two to seek balance and union. Thus, on the outer level, we leave our parents to seek a mate with whom to be joined as one flesh. On the immediate inner level, we abandon any allegiance to the notion that our sex determines our personality, potential, or performance, and seek instead easy communion within, among all our parts and aspects, certain that while physically male or female, we are also inwardly as much the other, and that in the confident and open recognition of that lies balanced harmony of the whole. And, following a still deeper sense of this teaching, we leave behind or release the values and paradigms of our fathers which have convinced us of, and bogged us down in, a separative understanding of reality, and turn instead toward an understanding and *real*-ization of union and the unity of life or Life. Each of these levels or senses speaks of and to the other, and as we turn our attention to one, so will the rest reflect that. The universe is plutonic, remember, and we cannot make alterations at one level without witnessing change at all others.

What all this has to do with divorce in a literal sense is that if we accept the validity of divorce in our outer lives, we will have accepted it inwardly as well, and it is that which the teacher would have us not do. Is he then forbidding divorce? While no one can speak for him, I would suggest it was not his style to forbid anything. Rather, he would urge upon any of us contemplating divorce, or any other decision, to seek to understand the ramifications, in a plutonic universe, of our intentions, motivations, and alternative courses of action. The inner search for truth is a universal one, but too it is intensely personal, and as we have suggested earlier, no one can prescribe or proscribe any of the steps for us. We have to do what seems most right to us after careful reflection at the moment of decision, confident that we can honestly and earnestly do no other and that the Light ahead, if we are genuinely seeking to see it, will eventually come into our view.

The "Yes, But" Syndrome

As we begin to look upon our relationships with others, upon everyone and everything in our lives, as the manifestation of what we are within, nothing will continue to seem as once it did. Our old beliefs, as we come to recognize their inadequacy and erroneousness, will cease to serve to explain to us satisfactorily what we are experiencing, and there will be a period in our early development when nothing seems to make any sense at all. In the process of shedding our old skin, as it were like a snake, but not yet fully comfortable in or conversant with our new, and true, attire, we will feel ourselves out of place and out of touch, drifting between a sense of reality which we now know to have been inaccurate and a vision which we have not yet truly grasped. Consider a seventeenth century European on first being told that the earth is round and not flat as he had been taught. Inevitably, the new knowledge must change everything he used to believe, for none of the old explanations about the universe can stand before it. But before he has fully absorbed the meaning of this discovery, he will be beset by a variety of seemingly ridiculous questions -- do people on the other side walk upside-down?, what direction do trees grow "down there"?, and why don't things fall off the bottom? Still trying to apply his former framework to the revised picture, even though he may be aware

98

he is doing so, our man seeks to make sense of a round world in flat-world terms. And he will continue to do so until he has come to realize, to make real within him the knowledge, that the new information really does alter *everything*. But he cannot change as quickly as the need to change can be brought to his attention, and his old belief structure will hang on. In a very real sense, we here are in a like position. While we have concluded that nothing is as it seems, we still will continue to try to apply the old explanations. We are unfortunately susceptible to what we might call the "yes, but" syndrome, under whose influence we find ourselves thinking: yes, I agree that the concept of an insecure, threatening future is a product of my mistaken beliefs about time, society, and life generally, and, yes, I recognize that if I can fully rid myself of the latter the former too will dissolve, but still I must work today to provide for tomorrow's needs. Or again, yes, I know that threatening anger against me perceived in others is a manifestation of my own inner anxieties, and indeed my concern about my physical safety is predicated upon a misunderstanding of what I truly am, but still I must maintain my defenses against my enemies. Just in case. And of course so long as we leave the door open to that "just in case" eventuality, it will -- in a plutonic universe -- seem and therefore be real to us.

Seeing Holographically

Here we might be able to make use, for illustration purposes, of another device, called a hologram. As I understand it, not even the physicists who work with these things can fully explain how or why they perform as they do, but for our needs in this discussion it is enough to know that a hologram is a specially devised picture, somewhat like a photograph, which is unique in that any part of it contains the whole and in the fact that, if any part is changed, the whole is changed accordingly. Thus, if a hologram is cut in half, for example, a projection of the remaining half nonetheless produces a complete image of the whole, as would clearly not be the case if one were to cut in half an ordinary photographic slide; and, if even only one small part of the hologram is changed, not altered in size but in composition, then the whole image is changed too, the whole reflecting the change to the one part. In somewhat the same way can the change in vision which we are talking about be said to work on our perception of reality. If we try in this search for truth simply to apply the lessons to our existing belief structure, perhaps in an effort to live a more "pious" life, our reality will still seem and be much the same as before, for while we may have abandoned some of our old practices, we will not have altered the basic framework of our lives -- in holographic terms, we will have cut in half the hologram, but the projected image remains unchanged. On the other hand, if we can succeed in seeing even one small part of our lives with the eyes of clear vision if only for just a moment, we will find that everything else looks different to us as well, for having altered one part of the hologram, the whole is changed. Unfortunately, as we have already observed, we are not entirely like the hologram, which once altered remains altered. Unless fully alert, we tend to slip back to the old ways, but fortunately it is also true that once we see even one small element of life as it truly is, we seem generally to be sufficiently moved by the event as never again to be long satisfied with or fully fooled by the illusion. Perhaps it can be said that while it is true that we are prone to back - sliding, we do not ever lose quite as much ground as we gained, and thus even in our seemingly inadequate struggling there is always progress.

But still, the commitment must be to total change. As we have said, it is not enough, nor is it possible, to try to live in both worlds. Armed, however tentatively at first, with the discovery that the world is not flat but round, we must be ready to get underway with a corresponding whole new set of charts and leave at the pier all the old precautions and safeguards developed earlier against falling off the edge. As the New Testament teacher put it, we cannot serve two masters. Once we have begun this spiritual unfoldment, this quest for Truth, nothing less will suffice, nor really feel right, than a determination to see it through to the end, whatever the cost -- and in a this-world sense, the cost is high including in the price as it does everything we now believe about everything. Whatever may have been the primary, driving purpose of our lives heretofore, our new focus must be to seek the Truth and all our activities must be seen as ways or means to accomplish or facilitate that effort. Thus, we may for example continue our former professions, but not as doctors, farmers, or bus drivers who seek, but as seekers who doctor, farm, or drive buses. Not as spouses or parents who seek, but as seekers who are parents or spouses. The seeking, then, is first, and becomes the motivating force behind, the purpose for, and the environment of everything else. And, to the extent that we are thorough in this endeavor, we will discover that we enjoy more and are much better at some of what we used to do. Only some I say, because much we will discard as no longer relevant or contributory. With fear, anxiety, and the threat of insecurity less the underlying foundations of our lives, we will find it easier to walk when we used to run, to embrace whom we used to grab, and to flow with what we used to struggle. And while there is more to this pilgrimage home than that, more that cannot be spoken because what *it* is, language isn't, this is a way to it. Our first step must be to come to terms with the knowledge that we are not what we think ourselves to be and neither is reality, that our neighbors, relationships, and experiences speak to us of much more than we now hear, for in a plutonic universe our beliefs, our lives, and we, and everything else, are not many but one, and the sooner we see that, the sooner we see.

THE REST WILL FOLLOW

We have removed our shoes. And by now, as we have been backing and forthing during this discussion over the past few chapters, the dust will have come up between our toes, and possibly we have even been shuffling and kicking around enough in the dirt below that our feet are nicely soiled, such that it may be difficult to tell anymore just where the soles end and the ground begins. That's good, because, as we have said, it is just those kinds of limitations, boundaries, and labels that we hope at first to fuzz up a bit and eventually to erase altogether. Especially the idea that God and His Things are somehow limited either by their nature or by some sense of propriety and blasphemy to specially selected, anointed, and created times or places. Or people.

Creating Our Reality

Everything we do or say or think or dream of doing; everything we believe about ourselves and everyone else; whatever we consider to be the nature of God and our relationship to Him (and atheists are not excused here, for to deny the existence of a thing is to acknowledge the thought about it, and as we have seen, it is at least at this point our thoughts that count); however we perceive and react to what we think is the reality within and around us -- all this determines who we are, and we are doing some of that *all the time.* So, wherever and whenever we are, at any instant, we are creating our reality. We are determining by all the choices (and remember, the choice not to choose *is* a choice) we make about everything the kinds of lives we will lead and, more importantly, whether we will lead them or be led by them. When God said to Moses, in effect, wherever you are, I am, He meant that to mean not just physically -- wherever we may be situated or located in space -- but mentally, philosophically, and psychologically as well. This is very much the same principle, and let's not be surprised at this, as is found in the question, who do you say I am?, or in the statement, I am who you say I am. There may be more to all of them than just this idea, but reaching for an understanding of this aspect will lead us toward the rest, for this is one of the ways to get there.

Our every thought, word, or deed creates. And it is not true that we can reserve our creative energies for so-called creative moments. We are always creating. Our reality is in a constant state of dynamic readiness and flux, looking directly to and at us for its shape and direction. We create it whether we like that fact or not, whether we are aware of it or not, even whether or not we would just as soon leave it to others. (Perhaps another aspect of God's remark about our standing on holy ground relates to this principle, that wherever we are we are creating, and there is surely no holier act than that.) For the one choice we cannot make seems to be this: in a plutonic universe, our choices determine our reality, but we do not, it would seem, have the choice *not* to make the choice, even though we may think we are doing so by abdication or in ignorance. We cannot change that fact because we did not create the universe; God did. And thank God for that, for while it is a universe which seems to permit us to be wrong about it and thus to manufacture for ourselves an ever-worsening and unpleasant reality, so is it a universe which responds just as quickly, effectively, and evidently to our efforts to see and be right about it. Make your choices, and the rest will follow. And if ever you forget or are in doubt about what choices you have made, look around you and ask yourself what it is you see. The answer to that question is your choice.

Look For The Judas

Once again, every choice we make determines our reality. Every choice. This point cannot be overemphasized, nor can it be said too often. If the repetition bores or angers you it is likely because you have still not really taken off your shoes, still not fully acknowledged that there is no time and no-where to which this principle does not apply.

There is an old joke about a fellow who, suffering from terrible headaches, goes from doctor to doctor in search of a cure, but of all the potions and remedies prescribed and tried, none works, and the incessant pain continues unabated. One day, in need of a new pair of shoes, he ventures into a shoestore and asks the salesman for a model in a particular size. The salesman, having measured the fellow's feet as a matter of course when he first sat down, responds that he would be glad to bring out the model requested, but recommends to the customer a half size larger. "But I've always worn this size," our friend insists. "Suit yourself," the salesman replies, "but, mark my words, they'll give you terrible headaches." Take off your shoes, for where you stand right now is where it all begins from now on. And that is true of every moment; our every choice determines our every thing. It is an awareness of this principle which we want to nourish and foster within us so thoroughly that each time, just before we speak, or think, or act, we will be reminded that we are about to make a choice. An automatic warning device that buzzes and clangs if necessary to get our attention and to focus our consciousness on the question: are we aware that whatever else we may think is going on, we are about to make a choice. That internal, self-activating alarm is the Judas within us, and he may be our best ally in our determination to see.

We are all, I expect, familiar with the Judas story. Even those who have not read the New Testament know of it, for his role in the account has become part of our language and culture. As I see it, however, few elements in the Gospels may have been as misunderstood or so thoroughly maligned, to *our* loss. It was Judas, you will remember, who turned in the teacher to the authorities; and that is generally about as far as we go with it, concluding therefrom that Judas was a traitor. But look at it instead this way for a moment: it was Judas who forced the issue. His action demanded of the teacher that he take a stand -- the final, ultimate stand for or against what he himself believed and had taught so effectively. Because of what Judas had done, the moment of truth was at hand. The teacher was fully aware of this, as his magnificent soliloquy in the garden makes abundantly clear. Would he run, fight, or negotiate with his accusers? All of these options, and perhaps others, were open to him. Struggling over which way to turn, as should we with each choice we make, the teacher chose none of those this-world solutions because he knew that each of them would keep him tied to this world. If he feared for his mortal life and acted accordingly, it could only be because he still believed in it, believed he was it, and that its loss was his loss -- (although he did waver for just an instant in what may be one of the most comforting and reassuring gifts of compassion to the rest of us struggling seekers stumbling along behind him!). Seeing the situation clearly and entirely for what it was -- an opportunity to opt again for the erroneous reality based upon a misunderstanding of the image in the prism, or to reach unreservedly for the Light -- he made his decision for the latter. As the seeker he was, he chose Life knowing that it would, that it must by definition, cost him his life. And it was Judas who brought that moment upon him.

To the rest of us left behind, of course, Judas is the betrayer precisely because it was he who cost the teacher what we still value most, life (in the lower case). Still believing the teacher to have been a man as we think ourselves to be, even though he repeatedly tried to tell us that he was not and that neither are we, we condemn Judas for bringing to the teacher's awareness what we do not seem to want brought to our own. Take off your shoes, Judas tells us, for we are, right this instant, every instant, about to make another choice, and every choice is *the* choice. Let us at least be aware of that, and not curse the alarm that awakens us! Even though we may choose to ignore it over and over again, let us urge it, nay pray for it, to do what it must do.

Before The Cock Crows

Time and again, with repeated frequency and increasing clarity, as we labor along the path to vision, will we hear the Judas within us alerting us to what we more and more know to be true. Still we will from time to time be deaf to the call, or, if hearing it, ignore it. Not this time, we will say, or not as regards this matter. We have been a long time, and covered much ground, in getting to just where we are now; the pressures and influences to carry on as before will be intense, and so will the apparent benefits to giving in seem real. We are, most of us, like the proverbial old dog in this act, and we learn slowly and often only begrudgingly, even though at base we know where our best interests lie, ahead. None knew this better than the teacher, for he too had been where we are now. Repeatedly he warned us of the risk and danger of backsliding. And in doing so, he never intended to impose guilt, only to impart awareness. The teacher knew that a sense of guilt, like error, shades the eyes, and it was clarity of vision that he was after. Hate not yourself, he would tell us, but rather the errors you have generated and adopted about yourself.

Before the cock crows (perhaps everywhere a symbol for dawn, itself a time-honored representation of the new awakening), the teacher observed, we will deny the Truth three times, which we here can understand to mean often. This was no threat, neither was it a curse, but simply the advice of a loving teacher to a struggling student. Like the disciple to whom that remark was offered, we will loudly and proudly protest the certainty and constancy of our determination, and then, again like him, we will falter. Still not fully disengaged from the value structure of our youth, having not yet completely released the ties to the old paradigms, we will choose to run, fight, or negotiate.

It Is Finished

But the end will come. In a moment which we can imagine and describe only from error erroneously, we will reject the illusion we have created from the image in the prism and become again what we always have been. What exactly that is, and how it happens, we cannot know, because the we who would know is the we to whom it must happen. Somehow, somewhere, just as we fell, we rise again. Having made the choice, and acted on it, to rid ourselves of all the shades, blinders, and lenses which befog, confuse, and distort our vision, and from which we have created an illusion out of Truth, we do so and it is done. The error, finally, ultimately, and clearly, seen for what it is and always has been, strung up before us as and in ourselves, the ourselves we thought ourselves to be, is erased and seen never to have been there at all. What never really was, at least not as we thought it was, is finally again seen as not being. Seen by what? Again, we cannot know because we are ourselves as we now think of ourselves part of the problem, and therefore whatever words we use now must fall short of the mark, serving at best as a signpost which points in the direction we should look but beyond which none of our logic or labels work. And how does a we which cannot go there get there? Recognizing that any answer we might attempt to develop to that question must perforce be in this-world terms and thus hopelessly inadequate (not to mention wrong), we deny any possibility of understanding how or why and simply rest assured that somehow it is done. By the grace of God.

Now, we must not confuse this final prism-smashing instant with physical death, even though in the New Testament the two seem to be the same event. On various occasions the teacher made quite clear the point that we need not die in the physical sense to see the Light, and indeed we should see physical death itself, being decidedly this-worldly, as simply another manifestation of our confused and mistaken interpretation of life and Life. Whatever else physical death may be or we may say about it, it seems clear enough that it is an activity that takes place on this side of the prism, and thus I suspect that it is not a ready way out of the cosmic bind we have gotten ourselves into. One way or the other, we are still left with the personal responsibility of having to recognize and to release the attachment we have permitted ourselves to develop to the false and erroneous view (which includes physical death) of Life.

Perhaps we have identified the act, or better, but equally hollow, the phenomenon by which the individual, separate and separative personality is subsumed by and re-united with the One, as death because we are ourselves, as we understand ourselves, so identified with that personality that we cannot imagine anything worse than its demise. Death seems to us the end of ourselves in the physical sense -- the only sense the old paradigms acknowledge -- and so we equate it with the end of ourselves in the parable or symbolic sense as well. We say the teacher died on the cross because that is what we saw happen, but in fact he "died" when he ceased to exist as a separate and separative personality, which he did when he withdrew his allegiance to and identification with his self as described and defined in this world terms. Does that mean he was erased or annihilated somehow, wiped clean off the slate without a trace? We cannot know, of course, but more likely it is simply that from here he stepped, or was lifted, beyond the bounds of our definitions and categories. What "happened", then, is precisely what we seek for ourselves, but still, unable to get a grasp on it, we fear it. Thus, the instant of our best possible good -- the final and full reawakening to who and what we truly are -- we have equated with the worst possible alternative as we see it now, physical death, precisely because we have forgotten or are wrong about who and what we really are and about what was going on at Calvary. As the teacher himself said, we did not then know what we were doing, and, he might have added, seeing. And too often we still don't. But now, on the mountain ourselves, our shoes off, feet in the mud and head in the clouds, we may be beginning to get a feel for it, as we allow that in its parable form, the death on the cross may have been intended to represent the body and all that we have let and encouraged it to become and mean for us, on display to be seen for what it is, and isn't.

Once Again, What's In A Name?

We said at the outset of this book that this would be a discussion between us, that there was, in effect, no point in my simply talking at you and your rendering "yea" or "nay" verdicts to ideas or thoughts as they arose in print. From an exercise of that kind nothing would be gained by either of us.

The teacher said that when two or more of us are gathered together in his name, he too would be there. Surely one of the intended lessons in that promise is the concept that when we gather together to seek an awareness of our true nature, and thus of Truth, Truth will come to us. From our struggling earnestly to see it, it manifests within us, and we see it, if only a little at a time. Accordingly, as we seek to know our own nature, as we join in that effort, it seems to happen. After all, the instant two or more of us agree on the possibility, however hesitantly or hypothetically at first, that the true nature of life may be that what seems to be two or more is actually somehow one, that where one of us ends and the other begins may be a line less easily drawn than once we thought, then already the truth of the matter is in our midst. And in that sense the teacher truly is among us, because by our joining together to wrestle with these questions as he did, as it was his nature to do, we become of his nature. We may be still bound by the past, of course, but now, aware of those binds, we are ready to release them (just as it was we who tied them) if the search leads us to that.

The man and his lessons are his nature, are our nature, and they cannot be divorced from each other. He was not just a man who taught Truth because what he taught he was. He was the voice of Truth speaking Truth, and in that sense whenever we too seek to do the same, he is among us. Not the man Jesus (as we now think of men), although we can see it that way if it helps, but the nature of the man, the Truth that he was, the Truth of the Universe.

So, the teacher was a man and his name was Jesus. What he saw, what he taught, what he was and is, is Truth, and we call that Christ. Jesus Christ then is the nature of the universe: man as he truly is, aware of it, and living it. Man as Truth, man-*real*ized-Truth; the creature seeing and being as the Creator sees and is. And that, it seems to me, is the lesson.

He said that we will all do as he did, and I believe we will, for I also believe that those words, like so many others of his, were a prediction and a promise, and, more, they were an affirmation, a statement of fact, perhaps *the* affirmation, about *the* nature of reality and of the universe.

A Few Final Words

Look inward. There is no more to any of this, to anyone's musings or teachings about the nature of reality than that. As Moses was assured, wherever he goes, God goes with him, and His voice is heard in the silence within. None of the world's true teachers, not Jesus nor any others, has said other than this, for there is nothing else to be said. And, as all of these great teachers have themselves taught, everything they might say or do is intended only to drive home for of us that truth.

116

Look inward. Gather what you can of your own thoughts and experiences and those of others, including these teachers, and take it home, within. There, seek to understand, and apply what you learn. There is no other way. You cannot walk where another has gone unless you take the steps yourself, unless *you* take them. From within.

To be sure, you will need teachers and guides. And they will be there, in various forms and guises, whenever you need them. Be alert to the need and you will recognize their presence. But never confuse their role with yours; they cannot do for you what you must do for yourself. They can and will point, push, and protect, but don't ask or expect of them more than is in the nature of the universe. Like your Creator, you are a creator. Accept that inescapable function with enthusiasm and humility, and you will never want for direction.

Life is a magnificent and awesome enterprise. It was intended to be joy-ful, and it is. Our failure to see that and thus to live it is simply a failure to see. It is a failure we can correct. Seek earnestly to do so, seek to see, and the rest will follow.

AUTHOR'S AFTERWORD

I hope that my decision to draw from the life and lessons of the man Jesus of Nazareth in the exploration and development of the ideas in this book will not suggest to anyone that he is alone a source for teachings in and of Truth. As I have tried to indicate numerous times, all of the world's great teachers and disciplines have pointed in the same direction, and every seeker, as he develops his own approach toward an understanding of the universe, would do well to feel free to look to each of them. There is available to us a wealth of guidance in various forms, and we would err grievously were we not to make use of it. From time to time, some will make sense and fit your needs, and some will not; you should make your choices accordingly. But don't ever let anyone else reach that determination for you. You are your own best teacher, and every true teacher will teach you that.

Regarding a more academic point, there may be among us some students of the New Testament who will want to point out that scholars believe that much, if not all, of the Gospel material as we have it now was written long after the physical death of Jesus and that indeed its inclusion in the Bible in preference, say, to other accounts of his life apparently also available, may have been based on factors and decisions less concerned with historical or religious accuracy than with other social, political, and related matters. Also, we know that what is now the Bible, has been transcribed and translated numerous times, and there is no way of determining how many changes, additions, or omissions the original texts may have suffered over the years. Finally, one might suggest that even if these objections are not valid, it still seems unlikely that any reporter, whoever it may actually have been who wrote these accounts for us, could remember so well so many of the man's actual words and the order and circumstances of their delivery. For my part, I am not sure just how relevant any of that is, except from an historian's point of view. I would suggest that what is important to us is whether or not the lessons can be applied to our own search for Truth. Their source is less significant than their effect, and none but we can determine that, and only for ourselves. Our concern, then, ought to be more about the direction in which they take us on our way home and less in how they happened to come to us along it. There is only one Truth. Whoever speaks it, however he words it and acts it out, if we genuinely seek to see it, we will, and that is all that matters.

SELECTED READING LIST

Like highway signs along a traveller's route, books can point. But where you are now and where you are headed will determine which sign best addresses your need at this moment.

One or more of these books may speak to you. On the other hand, they may not. It's just a list, after all.

Richard Bach *Illusions: The adventures of a reluctant Messiah.* Delacorte Press.

Sri Chinmoy *Beyond Within: A Collection of Writings.* Aum.

Ram Dass *The Only Dance There Is.* Anchor Books.

Foundation for Inner Peace *A Course in Miracles.*

Kahlil Gibran *Jesus: The Son of Man.* Knopf.

Christmas Huphreys *Walk on!.* Quest.

J. Krishnamurti *The Awakening of Intelligence.* Harper & Row

Lao Tsu *Tao Te Ching.* Vintage.

Thomas Merton *New Seeds of Contemplation.* New Directions.

Stefan C. Nadzo *There Is A Way.* Eden's Work.

Jack Schwarz *The Path of Action.* Dutton.

David Spangler *Reflections on the Christ.* Findhorn.

Teresa of Avila *The Interior Castle.* Any translation.

Chogyam Trungpa *Cutting Through Spiritual Materialism.* Shambhala.

Alan Watts *The Way of Zen.* Vintage.

Jay G. Williams *Yeshua Buddha.* Quest.